In this compelling book, Sam Cawthorn shares important life lessons that emerged from his extraordinary experience of overcoming adversity. Sam's inspiring message, conveyed with his characteristic clarity, charm and humour, will empower you to overcome obstacles and savour the joy of living every day.

— **Michael J. Gelb**
Author of *How to Think Like Leonardo da Vinci*

Sam has an inspirational story of 'life after death'. Sam lives his message and he is the most qualified to talk about this subject. This book has practical tips and advice to overcome any obstacle in life.

— **Dr V.S. Ramachandran**
Best-selling author and one of *Time* magazine's top 100 most influential people in the world

It's not often that a man comes back from the dead and lives to tell the tale but Sam is one of those miracle men.

— *The Telegraph*

T0052634

# HOW TO BOUNCE FORWARD

BE YOUR
**BEST**

# HOW TO BOUNCE FORWARD

**Change the Way You
Deal with Adversity**

## SAM CAWTHORN

# WILEY

First published as *Bounce Forward* in 2013 by John Wiley & Sons Australia, Ltd

42 McDougall St, Milton Qld 4064

Office also in Melbourne

This edition first published in 2020 by John Wiley & Sons Australia, Ltd

Typeset in 12.5/14.5pt Arno Pro

© Empowering Enterprizes Pty Ltd

The moral rights of the author have been asserted

ISBN: 978-0-730-38204-1

A catalogue record for this book is available from the National Library of Australia

Cover design by Wiley

Printed in USA by Quad/Graphics

V3DF8B919-C4FD-4C12-BE5B-D89C666341E4_103019

**Disclaimer**

The material in this publication is of the nature of general comment only, and does not represent professional advice. It is not intended to provide specific guidance for particular circumstances and it should not be relied on as the basis for any decision to take action or not take action on any matter which it covers. Readers should obtain professional advice where appropriate, before making any such decision. To the maximum extent permitted by law, the author and publisher disclaim all responsibility and liability to any person, arising directly or indirectly from any person taking or not taking action based on the information in this publication.

# Contents

# Preface

There are pivotal, game-changing moments in every person's life — the Greeks called them 'kairos moments'. For some those moments are so significant that they immediately fracture that life, ripping it forever into two parts — everything before that moment, and everything that came after.

My kairos moment occurred just after 3 pm on 3 October 2006. The day had started normally enough. I woke up early as usual, assisted by my eldest daughter Emelia, who was three and a half at the time. As the house stirred into life Milly (as we affectionately call her) left my wife, Kate, and me and went to wake up her little sister, Ebony, who was just 15 months old. The girls watched some cartoons as Kate prepared their breakfast and I got ready for work. It has been a Cawthorn family tradition that we all sit down at the table together, eat our breakfast and discuss our plans for the day. After breakfast the girls and I put on some loud music and danced around the living room. I would throw each one up in the air and catch her as she squealed and giggled with delight. I thought to myself how lucky I was and what a great way it was to start the day.

At the time I was working as an industry adviser to young people's trends and careers, like a youth futurist, an initiative funded by the Australian Federal Government. I'd been in the job only a few months but I loved it. I was 26 years old; I had a big job, good salary and great company car, plus I had a huge amount of freedom to work how I pleased. Essentially, my job was to follow cultural and economic trends so I could help predict how those trends would affect 13- to 19-year-olds entering the workforce. I would then liaise with employers and government to make sure young people were encouraged to move into industries and professions where there were job opportunities. I also watched for signs of market saturation so I could pass information back to the government, which would alert them to any likely reduction in new jobs in a particular industry or field.

I had a young family and a full-time job that sometimes required that I drive up to 1500 kilometres a week. I was also involved in my local community, running a youth group, and owned my own music studio where I taught hip-hop and singing. Life was *definitely* hectic.

As I climbed into my car — a white Holden V8 Statesman — Kate and the girls stood at the door to wave me off. There was a little L-shaped dent on the roof of the Statesman just above the driver's seat and Milly always thought it looked like a love heart. We felt it was a good omen of love and protection as I set off to work each day.

I had a couple of meetings and a lunch appointment in Burnie, about 150 kilometres from our home in Launceston in Tasmania, which is where I grew up and have spent most of my life. It was a little after three in the afternoon when I said goodbye to my lunch companions. I remember shaking hands, little knowing that this was the last right-handed handshake I would ever share. I began the journey home on the Bass Highway and about 10 minutes out of Devonport, a city half an hour from Burnie, near Parramatta Creek, I fell asleep at the wheel.

In a semi-conscious state I drifted across the road into the oncoming traffic. The driver of the truck I collided with thought I was trying to commit suicide. I wasn't. I was just exhausted from trying to keep so many balls in the air, and something had to give. What gave was the side of my Holden V8 Statesman sedan.

The first driver had successfully swerved out of the way, but the driver of the semi-trailer behind was not so lucky. Police estimated that upon impact, the truck driver and I were travelling at a combined speed of around 206 kilometres per hour. The first impact spun me around several times and ripped open the entire right side panel of the car. Within a fraction of a second another car, which had been travelling behind the truck, ploughed straight into me — and I mean straight *into* me. Without the side panel there was no protection whatsoever. I can still hear the terrible impact of that final collision.

That moment changed my life forever.

When the roaring of twisted metal finally came to a stop, there was absolute silence — at least I couldn't hear anything. I could see the damage but somehow it didn't register in my mind as being real. Smoke billowed from the carnage and I remember looking down at myself; I was a mess. I could see my bones and flesh exposed and there was blood everywhere. My right arm had been obliterated, the elbow was completely gone and my hand was attached to my arm by a thin thread, my right leg was completely shattered, and the pain was like nothing I've ever experienced!

Despite the late afternoon sun, I was very cold. 'HELP!' I yelled. 'GOD SAVE ME!' Every ounce of energy within me was trying to coordinate my breathing and my yelling. 'HELP, GOD, GOD, PLEEEEASE HELP ME, DON'T LET ME DIE TODAY. PLEASE TELL MY WIFE I LOVE HER.'

When Kate was told of the accident a friend rushed her to the hospital. Unfortunately there was only one way to get there and it meant driving past the scene of the accident. One of the worst moments of her life was recognising the little L-shaped love heart on the roof of the mangled Holden, and wondering how anyone could have escaped alive.

In truth, it was initially thought I didn't escape alive. Six months after the accident I was in a wheelchair having dinner at a restaurant and I was approached by a guy who wanted to know if I was the man from the Parramatta Creek accident. It turned out he was a coroner's taxi driver. He was informed that there had been a really bad accident on the Bass Highway and he was probably going to be needed to collect a body — mine! Thankfully the paramedics successfully resuscitated me when they arrived on the scene.

My right arm was destroyed, I broke six ribs, lacerated my liver, punctured my kidney and both lungs collapsed. I dislocated my hip; my entire quad muscle was ripped from the bone on my right leg. My cruciate ligaments had torn and I shattered my femur, knee cap, fibula and ankle and lost the nail on my right big toe. I was devastated at having lost my big toenail!

Yet as far as I am concerned I was incredibly lucky. First, no-one else was badly injured. Second, I was alive. My accident certainly changed my life, but as the Greek philosopher Epictetus once said, 'It's not what happens to you, but how you react to it that matters.'

So often people talk about 'bouncing back' after disaster, crisis, tough times or difficulty, but my body was broken. There was no way I could ever bounce back to the old Sam Cawthorn. It wasn't physically possible. I began to obsess about this idea and started to research resilience and how others had overcome incredible obstacles to pull off amazing comebacks.

In countless cases individuals and businesses used great challenges to forge ahead and create a better life or create even greater success.

Nothing in life stays the same for long. Change and challenge are constant, although the speed and complexity of change now means we can expect upheaval every few years. World economies are still reeling from the global financial crisis that began in 2007–08. Business is getting tougher and tougher and yet there are still success stories everywhere you look. Clearly some people have already instinctively tapped into the power of bounce and learned how to use the inevitable difficulties of life as a springboard to something better.

No-one is immune to the challenges of life. Bad stuff happens to everyone regardless of wealth, background or education. For some their crisis will be professional — losing a major client, being made redundant or having to adapt to a changing market during an economic downturn. For others their crisis may be personal — the breakdown of a relationship, serious illness or, like me, physical injury. Pain is inevitable; it is part of being alive. But misery is optional. I knew I had a choice: I could give up, listen to the doctors who told me I'd never walk again, and wallow in misery and bitterness. Or I could accept that things had changed and use the crisis to reinvent myself and get better. I chose the latter. The challenges we face in life are not meant to be some sort of punishment; rather, they are an invitation to change — and an opportunity to create something even better than before.

Since my accident I have experienced excruciating pain but I have also become stronger, happier and more determined because of it. I have come to understand the transformational power of acceptance and have developed a process to help businesses, organisations, teams and individuals to go far beyond 'recovery' or 'bouncing back' to create revolutionary change by *bouncing forward* into greater joy and success.

Too often, when crisis knocks on our door — whether professional or personal — either we ignore it, or we use all our energy and resources to try to go back to the way things were. We scramble to fix the problem so either it goes away or life somehow goes back to the way it used to be.

I believe that the reason crisis sometimes destroys people or breaks their spirit is that they are fixated on what used to be. All their efforts are directed toward trying to recapture that experience or way of life. But sometimes there really is no going back. There is, however, *always* a way forward. I'm not promising that it's going to be easy, but this book is your road map through crisis so you can bounce forward into a better life.

Bounce consists of four crucial principles:

» Crisis creates opportunity.

» Proximity is power.

» Leverage positivity to fuel success.

» Bounce forward not back.

If you want to successfully navigate crisis and difficulty so you can use adversity to achieve even greater success, then you must understand these principles. Each of the four principles, as outlined in chapters 1–4, is facilitated by four habits. These habits may not come naturally to you, but if you focus on fostering each one in your daily life you will master crisis and learn how to consistently benefit from difficulty. Finally, once I've explained all four principles, in chapter 5 you will be invited to take the 12-day crisis turnaround challenge. This process will help get you into the right frame of mind to take action, to advance quickly through your current challenge by activating the power of the bounce principles.

Although I will focus mainly on bouncing forward in business and your career following redundancy or a career setback, bounce is as applicable to a personal crisis as it is to a professional one. You will learn about cutting-edge science and the research that underpins the bounce forward process, and how to use it to make real, long-lasting positive change — whether the problem you face is a minor irritant or a disaster so huge it has recalibrated your life forever.

My crisis demanded full recalibration. I lost my arm and I still have several physical limitations; I can't, for example, bend my right leg. But I honestly wouldn't change a thing. Everything that has happened in my life, including my accident, has made me the person I am today. In 2008, two years after my accident, Kate and I welcomed our son, Jacob, into our family and I now live a life I couldn't even have dreamed of before my accident.

And if I can do it, so can you. Remember, pain is inevitable — misery is optional. Forget about trying to recover what used to be. Instead embrace the crisis and use it to bounce forward into a life that is bigger, better and brighter than ever before.

# About the author

In 2006 Sam Cawthorn's life changed forever when he was involved in a major car accident which left him with an amputated right arm and permanent disability in his right leg. In a blistering demonstration of the process and mindset laid out in this book, Sam *Bounced Forward*, and went on to become one of the world's most in demand professional speakers.

Today, Sam is a successful entrepreneur. He is the CEO and founder of Speakers Institute, a training company that teaches the art and craft of professional speaking so others with powerful stories to share can master communication for maximum influence. The not-for-profit Speakers Tribe initiative then connects that community of speakers so they can change the world one message at a time.

Sam is the author of seven books including two international bestsellers — *Bounce Forward* and *Storyshowing*. He has been voted Young Australian of the Year and Edupreneur of the Year. The Edupreneur Awards are all about recognising and celebrating the positive contributions Edupreneurs make to the knowledge, skills and competencies of their market.

'After my near-death experience people wanted to hear my story to feel inspired. I've now reached over 170 million people in over 95 countries via my speaking engagements, social media and books.' — Sam Cawthorn, Speakers Institute Founder & CEO.

Sam is married to Kate, they have three children and currently live in Sydney, Australia.

Connect with Sam:

> Websites: www.samcawthorn.com and www.speakersinstitute.com

> Facebook, Skype & LinkedIn: Sam Cawthorn

> Twitter: www.twitter.com/samcawthorn

> Blog: www.samcawthorn.com/blog

# Acknowledgements

This book was written in honour of my brother David. You inspire me every day!

I would like to thank Karen McCreadie who was the backbone in putting this book together. My awesome wife Kate and my three children, Emelia, Ebony and Jacob. Lucy Raymond and the Wiley team who believed in me. Darren Hill for the inspiration of Bouncing Forward. My speaker friends who were instrumental in the journey. My father Peter, who inspires me every day of my life. I would also like to thank God, the reason why I live a passionate life.

# Introduction:
# **The Bounce Cycle**

The ancient Greeks had two words for time: *chronos* and *kairos*. *Chronos*, the source of the word 'chronological', refers to ordered or sequential time. *Kairos* refers to an indeterminate moment within time when something special happens. It's an interesting and fine distinction. For most of us, day-to-day life is just the passage of time, but then there are moments, days, weeks, months or even years that stand out as especially significant. This sort of time changes lives.

Change of any sort can be uncomfortable, confronting and painful. For the most part we automatically assume that change is difficult and should be avoided wherever possible. And yet who said that change was bad? Change is like the weather: it's inevitable and in itself is neither good nor bad— it just is. Rain is good for the farmer who needs it to grow his crop. If, however, you've saved all year to take your family to Disney World and it rains every day, then the same condition is far from welcome. Interestingly, *kairos* also means weather in both ancient and modern Greek.

Change for me came when I was fitted with the most advanced bionic arm in the world. Learning how to control the bionics in my arm has been a difficult change, yet looking back I realise that my bionic arm can do more and is stronger than my real arm ever was.

Our attitude to change essentially comes down to who initiates the change or how it is initiated. If we initiate the change, then it can be seen as positive and exciting. If change is thrust upon us, then it is rarely welcomed and seldom viewed optimistically. My kairos moment was most definitely thrust upon me; it started when my car smashed into a truck and ended several months later when I realised that not only was it not possible for me to go back to my old life, but that I genuinely didn't want to.

I didn't realise it at the time, but I'd entered the bounce cycle.

## Crisis

The first stage of the bounce cycle is the kairos moment of crisis — an event or situation that either occurs in an instant or creeps up on you over time. Either way you will know when you reach the crisis point as it will be seared into your consciousness forever.

In business these moments can take a multitude of different forms. Perhaps you've lost a major client or you've been informed of legislative change that will require massive reinvestment. Perhaps you've lost a key member of staff or your market share has dropped dramatically. Perhaps your business has received negative press and this has negatively affected sales. Whatever the cause, you are in crisis.

Immediately after my accident my body went into shock, but I wasn't really sure how bad it was because I couldn't move. Also,

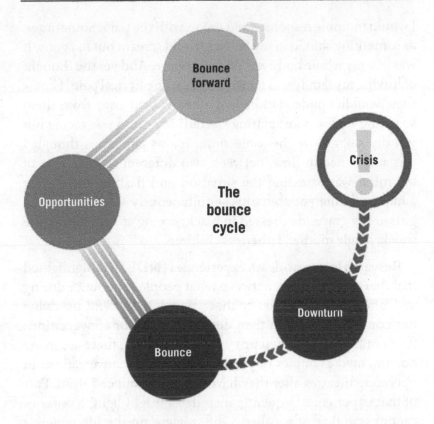

other motorists had stopped to see if they could help and I could tell by the looks on *their* faces that my situation was not terrific. When someone recoils in horror and puts their hand up to their mouth and gasps, wide-eyed, it's not terribly comforting.

Thankfully three women, whom I'll call Jane, Michelle and Sharon to protect their privacy, didn't recoil in horror and stayed with me until the paramedics arrived. They kept talking to me, asking me questions in an effort to keep me conscious. They asked me if I was married and whether I had children. If I answered with only one word they pushed for more information so I would not drift off. I told them about Kate and my two little girls and asked them to call Kate and tell her I loved her.

I would mumble responses and groan with the pain. Sometimes, as something shifted in my body, I would scream out in agony. It was like my whole body was one raw nerve. And yet the thought of leaving my family was far worse than the physical pain. I knew they wouldn't understand why I'd been taken away from them so young — I was just getting started! My mind was racing but weirdly sluggish at the same time. It was almost as though I was suspended in time, between two different worlds. Part of my mind was assessing the situation and flashing images for a hundred different scenarios simultaneously — Kate and the girls at my graveside dressed in black, crying at my funeral, the shock, single mother, fatherless children.

Research into near-death experiences (NDE) has highlighted that there is a similarity between what people experience during and 'after' death. Obviously these people don't end up dying but come back and can then describe events or conversations they could not have been privy to. For example, there are many documented examples of patients recounting conversations in operating theatres after they have been pronounced dead. Part of that experience frequently includes a bright light, a sense of calmness and what is called a 'life review'. In the life review a person will receive a panoramic view of their own life including everything they did and said and how their actions affected others.

For me it was slightly different. I did experience the bright light and the calmness, but the review didn't focus only on the past. I was thinking about everything — what life meant; my friends, my family and my whole life up until that point. I was calm and yet agitated. What could I have done differently? Why couldn't I have cherished my life more? Was this really the end? Would I have an opportunity to go back and change things? Why had I taken so much for granted? It's amazing how desperately you want to live when you are about to die.

## Downturn

This is the make-or-break point following a crisis! Decisive action needs to be taken in order to bounce. In many ways this is the most crucial time in the bounce cycle, because it simply won't be possible to bounce if the tough decisions are not made.

Some people don't make it past this point. Unable to see a life worth fighting for beyond the crisis, they accept defeat and immediately slip into downturn. Or they avoid the tough decisions and instead get 'busy', tinkering at the edges of the crisis. They convince themselves they are doing something but the something they are doing is too small or irrelevant to turn the monster. Fiddling around with little shifts and tweaks can simply prolong the crisis and stop you from bouncing, which means you slip into downturn anyway.

Downturn happens if you are either not being real about the situation or not making the tough decisions for drastic change! A downturn happens when you are not sufficiently prepared for the crisis and no mechanisms are in place to counteract the downturn or you have not taken decisive action. The bounce (the next one in the cycle) will happen only if the tough decisions are made.

Trapped in my wrecked car I was clearly badly injured and I was struggling to stay awake. I was exhausted and the pain was intense. I was in crisis — physically, emotionally and spiritually. My kairos moment had arrived. I couldn't ignore it. I couldn't think positively and pretend to myself that I wasn't in a mangled car fighting for my life. I had a very *real* problem and no amount of positive thinking, denial or pretending was going to change it. I was heartbroken at the thought of leaving my family. I felt overwhelmed by the sorrow and guilt I felt and I slipped into the darkness of downturn.

Downturn is the time between crisis and rock bottom. In the downturn you have only two choices. You can slide to rock bottom and hope the deeper crisis *that* causes creates enough momentum for change. Or you can choose to act sooner rather than later and use the distance and momentum between where you are now and rock bottom to bounce!

I chose the latter. I chose to fight and I chose to live. I decided in that moment that I would become a living demonstration of the transformational power of bouncing forward, although I didn't call it this at the time.

## Bounce

This stage of the bounce cycle is the turning point. But it's also the toughest time because it's the lowest point of the cycle.

That was certainly my experience. I'm not going to lie — it took everything I had to fight. The pain was brutal and it would have been much easier to surrender to the calmness and drift off to sleep, but I wanted to live. Jane, Michelle and Sharon were still with me, encouraging me to talk. Sharon kept repeating to me over and over again, 'Sam, just keep breathing, breathe in, breathe out, just keep breathing and you'll be okay.' It was great advice and I dragged all my attention and focus to the simple rhythmic act of breathing. Unknown to me at the time both my lungs were collapsing so breathing was neither simple nor rhythmic but it was essential if I was to survive. Besides it didn't require me to move too much so I obsessed about this one small act.

I'm not sure how long I was in the wreckage but I know if it wasn't for those three women who stopped to help I wouldn't have made it.

Paramedics arrived on the scene together with firefighters who brought the 'jaws-of-life', a hydraulic tool used to force or cut open wrecked cars so the trapped occupants can be extracted. I don't remember much about this time, but I do remember the jaws-of-life — it was horrendous. It was very difficult for the paramedics to know where my body ended and the car began and vice versa. It felt like it took forever for them to work out how to free me and then get the jaws into the right position so they could make a cut to the car. Because I was literally part of the car I felt every cut, and the sound of grinding metal was almost as bad as the pain caused by each incision. Little by little the car was prised away from my body. It was obviously appallingly painful but I realise that pain was a necessary part of the crisis process. I needed to push through that pain to get to the new life on the other side. I was being broken free of the car but at the same time I was breaking free of my past too. The last thing I remember was being pulled from the wreckage, then everything went black.

## Beyond the change curve

Each crisis takes a different form but the process of transition remains much the same. In 1969 Swiss-American psychiatrist and near-death studies pioneer Elisabeth Kübler-Ross wrote a book called *On Death and Dying*. In this book she proposed that everyone faced with the news of their impending death will move through five distinct stages of grief:

1. denial
2. anger
3. bargaining
4. depression
5. acceptance.

The Kübler-Ross Model revolutionised medical care for terminally ill patients and she later expanded her theoretical model so it might be applied to any form of dramatic change. Not everyone who experiences a life-threatening or life-altering event experiences each stage or necessarily transitions through the stages in this order, but the model has become a widely accepted and much- used framework to guide people through major crisis.

In business this model is known as the *change curve* and often contains additional stages including initial shock, which usually precedes denial, and integration, which usually follows acceptance.

After the crash I was most definitely in shock. My first real memory after the blackout was looking across and seeing my mother sitting by my bedside. She tried to explain to me what had happened — that I'd been involved in a car accident and I was in intensive care. But by then I had moved into denial, assisted by vast quantities of pain medication. I remember looking at her and she was telling me about my arm but all I kept thinking was that I needed to take Kate out for coffee in Paris. (Later my medical team told me they had been talking to me about 'plaster of Paris'!) Denial can be a useful mind trick to get you through the initial trauma of a crisis, so long as you don't stay there for too long.

I think it's the mind's way of helping you cope. Think of crisis as a door that needs to be opened. Denial will gently open the door a fraction and let you imagine that it's still closed for a little while. If that door had been flung open immediately and I'd fully registered the extent of my injuries, I might have extinguished the bounce I had experienced when I decided to fight and have gone into freefall, slipping back to downturn.

By the time I opened my eyes I had been in a coma for six days. I was obviously heavily medicated, which went some way to explaining the elephants parading around the walls of my hospital room and the water seeping from the ceiling, falling on me and running off to create rivers on the floor! One minute I would be talking to Kate and the next I would be alone in my room wondering why I was there. Everything was disjointed. I don't know when I realised I'd been injured. Maybe I always knew it but didn't want to admit it.

As the drugs wore off and my body started to heal I became more alert. With my awareness returning the door opened more fully and I began to acknowledge what Kate and my mother were telling me. I was seriously hurt. My injuries were horrific: the crash had broken and mangled my body. My right arm had been amputated midway between my elbow and shoulder, but all I could see were the dressings and where my arm now ended. Seeing that was a shock.

They kept me largely immobilised at first to prevent me from injuring myself further. I was hooked up to various monitors via endless tubes and wires, and my right leg was encased in a metal frame that passed through my leg to hold the bones together — it was inside and outside my leg at the same time. That was also a shock. Just looking at it made me feel queasy!

I can honestly say I didn't experience anger. It wasn't like it was anyone else's fault, and frankly even if it had been what would have been the point of getting mad about it? It wouldn't bring my arm back. I didn't think there was much point bargaining either. The extent of my injuries was pretty clear. I'd even been told I probably wouldn't walk again. That information floored me again and made me feel sad for the first time. I just couldn't shake the feeling that I'd let my family down. I couldn't see how I could contribute to their world if I was so badly injured. Kate hadn't worked since having our girls. I was the breadwinner. How were we going to manage if I couldn't even walk?

At this point the only people I'd seen were Kate and my mother; I hadn't yet seen the rest of my family or my friends.

And while they had both been very sensitive, I didn't know what they really thought of me now. I wasn't depressed but I was definitely morose! Lying there in that hospital bed, I was pretty gloomy. It wasn't just about my ability to provide for my family or even my injuries, but the doctors' prognosis meant I'd never play with my kids again. Never run alongside them or go swimming with them. It was just so demoralising. I didn't want to be a burden to them. I didn't want them to grow up looking after their disabled dad, pushing me along in my wheelchair. That was my first real insight into just how much my life had changed.

Thankfully I didn't stay morose for very long. And I have my family, my friends and my faith to thank for that. I remember very clearly the moment I bounced into the fourth stage of the bounce cycle.

## Opportunities

Kate had deliberately kept our daughters, Milly and Ebony, away from the hospital because she didn't want to scare them. Ebony was still very young, but Milly was keen to come and visit and a few days after I woke up we decided it was time. I'll never forget that day. I heard Milly skipping along the corridor and singing to herself and I propped myself up in the bed as best I could. I don't mind admitting I was terrified. What would she think? How would she react to me? I didn't know if she would panic. I didn't look the same anymore. I was enveloped in tubes, my arm was missing and my leg was in a metal cage! What would happen if she didn't accept me? I wasn't sure if I could cope with that. I'd already been through the mill stressing about how I was going to provide for them all and how I was going to be a good dad — what would I do if she couldn't even look at me? The last time I'd seen her was the morning of the accident. We'd been dancing in the living room, with me throwing her up in the air and catching her as she screamed and giggled. I'd never be able to do that again.

Before I had time to gather my thoughts she was outside the door. I heard her stop and she went quiet. I didn't move a muscle. I then saw two tiny little hands grab hold of the door from the side, and she peered into the room. A moment later she burst in and climbed up on the bed. 'Daddy! Daddy! Daddy!' She didn't care that I was a bit broken; she still accepted me and I knew that everything would be alright. I was still Daddy and I was ALIVE!

My little girl brought laughter back into that hospital room and bounced me forward. Although I wasn't able to move and hug her it was so wonderful to see her little face. As usual she launched into a thousand questions. 'Daddy! Daddy! Daddy! Did you have a car accident?' I nodded. 'Daddy, Daddy, Daddy! Did you lose your arm in the accident?' I said, 'Yes, I lost my arm.' Then she looked me straight in the eye, with that serious expression only a three- and-a-half-year-old can pull off. 'And Daddy, the doctors looked for your arm but they couldn't find it anywhere!'

After the accident Milly had overheard a conversation between Kate and the police about my having lost my arm. She had thought that meant that it had fallen off and I couldn't remember where I'd put it. As she explained this to me everyone in the room laughed.

Apparently people were looking for it now and the doctors had better have sticky tape with them when they found it so they could make me better again, 'because, Daddy, sticky tape fixes *everything!*'

Interestingly, the more my mood lifted and the more optimistic and determined I became to seek opportunities and bounce into a better life, the more sombre my doctors became. They say when life gives you lemons, make lemonade. Well I went into lemonade production overdrive and my doctors were seriously concerned that I wasn't accepting the reality of my situation. I clearly wasn't cycling through the change curve as expected.

It may be that for some forms of crisis denial can work for a long time. It's certainly possible to stick your head in the sand if your sales are down or if you've lost a major client, but there is something very real about physical injury that makes denial a little silly. I had accepted my accident. I knew that my life was different now and that I needed to find a different path and new solutions to various very real and tangible problems, such as how I was going to make a living. But I genuinely didn't see why I had to be miserable about it. Pain is inevitable and facing months of agonising physiotherapy I was fully aware of that, but I was determined that misery didn't need to accompany it. I didn't want to be one of those people who just gave up on life.

As the weeks turned into months and my physical recovery continued they kept expecting my optimism to crack. I was warned over and over again that it was a mask or shield that my mind had created to protect me from the trauma that had occurred. On more than one occasion the doctors told me that it was okay to feel upset or depressed, that it happened to everyone eventually. They'd say things like, 'Look Sam, we've seen you adopt this façade of happiness and your rehabilitation is going well, but you will hit a brick wall so you need to be ready for the inevitable dark times that will follow.' It was as though they were trying to talk me into it! And the more they tried, the more I was determined to prove them wrong.

I didn't accept that my optimism was a mask I wore to prevent people from knowing my real feelings. To me, I'd been given a second chance. My family loved me unconditionally. I was alive. I would find a way to walk and I'd adapt to losing my arm. No matter what condition I was in, it was my decision that determined who I was and the life I wanted to live. No-one else was injured. I was still me; no-one was going to tell me who I was or the life I was going to live — that was my choice. I might look a little different but my spirit wasn't damaged, just my body. These simple realities gave me hope and fuelled my determination to press on and break through any barriers that blocked my way.

## Bounce forward

In his book *Halftime* American author and businessman Bob Buford tells his story. In the first half of his life Buford was the president and CEO of a tremendously successful cable TV company. He enjoyed a happy marriage and a loving relationship with his only son. He had good friends and loved his life, yet he couldn't shake a gnawing feeling that something was missing. At 44 Buford recalls experiencing 'success panic' — 'a quiet, insidious intruder, disturbing the dark peace and slinking about at the trappings of life overflowing with contentment, money, achievement, and energy'. Suddenly he began to look at his life differently: the accumulation and drive for success phase was over, and he craved something deeper and more meaningful. This sense of unease and growing dissatisfaction was brought to a head with the sudden tragic death of his only child. Needless to say, Buford and his wife were devastated. Their loss pushed them both into what he calls 'half-time'. In the same way that a football or basketball game has half-time, Buford suggests that every life also has a half-time when we must assess the first half to see if we are happy with our performance. If not, then we have the second half to put it right.

When I read *Halftime* it really struck a chord with me. Management guru Peter Drucker, a friend of Buford's, said, 'The biggest discovery in half time is that all of us have more than one life to live. And the opportunity we have in half time is to regain control of our lives and reallocate them to something that's more about meaning than money.'

Buford had already been experiencing 'success panic', otherwise known as a midlife crisis. When he lost his son in a drowning accident his life was turned upside down. In the hours of darkness that followed he found himself in conversation with a strategic consultant who asked him, 'What's in the box?' When it comes to success in business or in life there is one central idea that guides everything, and that central idea is what needs to be in the box. Coca-Cola, for example, thought their central idea was 'great taste' and this idea persuaded them to tamper with the recipe and create New Coke, which was a corporate disaster. What was really in the box for Coke was 'American tradition', and no company in its right mind would tamper with that. Once this consultant helped them realise what was really in the box New Coke was swiftly removed from the market. In the same way, Buford was encouraged to decide what was in his box and put that front and centre in his life. By doing so he was able to shift his focus from success to significance and make a difference to other people's lives. And, despite his grief, his life was transformed as a result.

I may not have realised it at the time, but my accident called half- time on my life, even though I was just 26. My focus and current direction was not where it needed to be. I had no compelling purpose in life — I had forgotten my *why*, or perhaps I'd never really known it. I'll explain this idea more fully in chapter 1, but I believe that we all have a purpose and everything we do begins with that 'why'.

**THERE IS ONE THING THAT WE ALL MUST DO. IF WE DO EVERYTHING ELSE BUT THAT ONE THING, WE ARE LOST. AND IF WE DO NOTHING ELSE BUT THAT ONE THING, WE WILL HAVE LIVED A GLORIOUS LIFE.**

**— RUMI**

Some may live a life skirting around their purpose, some may never find their why, some may know it but refuse to take action on it, and some just forget it or give up on it. My accident was a genuine blessing to me because it forced me to fully connect to my purpose, which has transformed my life. I knew I was going to get better. I was going to work again. I wasn't just going to survive — I was going to find a way to thrive. And once I did I was going to help others to navigate the bounce cycle so they could bounce forward into a better life, regardless of the crisis they face.

Having experienced the sharp end of crisis I have a greater understanding of and appreciation for the change curve. I think it's a pretty useful tool as long as you don't become limited by it. Its power is in helping people to understand the stages they *may* experience as they cycle through change and grief, so they don't feel isolated and alone. But none of the stages are compulsory. You don't need to get angry and you don't need to waste time bargaining if you don't want to. But perhaps the biggest limitation of the model is that it implies that the best we can hope for is acceptance. Acceptance is absolutely not the final destination! For me, it's the point after acceptance that determines the trajectory of a life or a business. Acceptance is far too passive. It implies that when crisis visits the best we can hope for is a quiet resignation to the inevitable change it brings.

I knew I wasn't the only person in the world who had experienced a crisis and refused to accept mediocrity as the outcome, that there were others out there who had used crisis as a springboard to greater things. Bouncing back was too limiting. I didn't want my old life. I wanted something better — for me and my family.

I became obsessed with this idea and started to deconstruct the mechanics of bounce forward so I could help others to successfully navigate a crisis through the bounce cycle. When you bounce forward, acceptance isn't an end point from which you mourn a life once lived; it's merely a stage toward a bigger, better and brighter life.

The first four chapters document the bounce principles that can ensure that your crisis makes you a happier, stronger and more productive individual or a happier, stronger and more productive business.

# Part I
# **The bounce principles**

# CHAPTER 1
# Principle 1: Crisis creates opportunity

In 1959 John F. Kennedy delivered a speech in which he said, 'When written in Chinese the word *crisis* is composed of two characters. One represents danger, and the other represents opportunity.' Since then this insight has entered popular culture and is widely used in politics and business and by inspirational speakers the world over.

There is no doubt that crisis presents both danger and opportunity, but this much-loved interpretation isn't actually accurate. A more faithful translation of the two characters that make up the Chinese symbol for crisis would be 'danger' and 'crucial point'. Most people take crisis to involve some sort of personal or professional emergency that must be weathered. It doesn't. At least it doesn't have to. If you look up *crisis* in your dictionary you will find that the definition usually refers to a 'crucial or decisive moment or turning point'. In fact, the word itself comes from the Greek word *krinein* — to decide. A crisis therefore is a call to action — a situation or event that demands your attention and forces you to decide how to react and what to choose for yourself going forward.

Events, situations and circumstances do not in themselves create crisis. What creates the danger that is inherent in crisis is an unwillingness to face the truth and take constructive action to change the outcome.

For example, when it comes to a crisis, they don't come much bigger, certainly in living memory, than the global financial crisis (GFC). Since it began toward the end of 2007 the GFC has caused unprecedented financial destruction to international stock markets, countries, businesses, governments and individuals. The meltdown that occurred between 2007 and 2012 is considered by many leading economists to be the worst financial disaster since the Great Depression of the 1930s. And yet, according to the *World Wealth Report 2010* published by Merrill Lynch and Capgemini, there was a 34 per cent increase in Australian millionaires between the end of 2008 and the end of 2009. By the end of 2008 there were 129 200 individuals in Australia with net assets, excluding their home, of at least $1 million. By the end of 2009 there were 173 600 such individuals. The year 2007 may have marked the beginning of the GFC, but it also marked the end of one of the longest economic booms in living memory. In other words, crisis? What crisis? For some 44 400 people crisis created opportunity and they bucked the negative trend to come out on top.

And these individuals are not alone. Some of the most successful businesses in the world started out during an economic downturn of some type, including Procter & Gamble, CNN, Hyatt Hotels, Kraft Foods, Disney, Revlon and IBM. The US publication dedicated to wealth, *Fortune* magazine, was launched during the Great Depression.

Even the technology powerhouse Apple has weathered a few considerable economic storms. Although Apple started life in

1976 it didn't move into hyperdrive until the middle of the dot.com crash. When all things tech were considered bad news Apple's Steve Jobs instructed his team of engineers to develop a personal music player, and the iPod was created in less than a year.

Launched in November 2001, it became an instant hit. Two years later Apple launched iTunes, and the rest is history. The iPhone and iPad followed, and who knows what funky new 'must have' products they will create in the future. All because they refused to see the crisis and focused on innovation.

Still more recently, Groupon, the online 'deal-of-the-day' discount coupon company, started life in November 2008 during the GFC. What better time to launch a business that offered people the opportunity to buy stuff at a discount price? Within the space of two years Groupon had reached more than 200 markets worldwide and was reported to have some 35 million registered users seeking discount deals. In 2011 Google offered $6 billion for the business. The GFC created a phenomenal opportunity for this business. According to *Forbes* magazine and *The Wall Street Journal*, at projected revenue Groupon was on target to make $1 billion in sales faster than any other business in history.

A 2009 study conducted by the Ewing Marion Kauffman Foundation, 'The Economic Future Just Happened', concluded that challenging economic times can inspire entrepreneurial rebirth. In fact, the study found that 'more than half of the companies on the 2009 *Fortune* 500 list were launched during a recession or bear market, along with nearly half of the firms on the 2008 *Inc.* list of America's fastest-growing companies'.

Obviously, crisis isn't always negative. Crises simply force us to look outside our comfort zone and actively seek opportunities that were probably there the whole time. When life is easy and times are good we don't see these opportunities because we don't need to. This is not just common sense — it's biological too.

## The biology of innovation

In *Eat, Fast and Live Longer*, a great documentary that aired on UK TV, British journalist, physician and TV presenter Dr Michael Mosley investigated the health benefits of fasting. In one particular segment of the show he visited Dr Mark Mattson, Chief of the Laboratory of Neurosciences at the National Institute on Aging in Baltimore, Maryland, USA, and professor of neuroscience at Johns Hopkins University. Dr Mattson was conducting some startling experiments on mice. The mice were fed different diets and released into a maze, where they needed to work out and remember where the food was. The mice fed a high-fat, western diet fared pretty badly: either they couldn't figure out where the food was or they could find it but later couldn't remember where it was. However, the mice fed one day and starved the next did really well. When the researchers examined the brains of the fasting mice they discovered something amazing — newly created brain cells. Sporadic bouts of hunger trigger the new neurons to grow, making the mice more resourceful and mentally focused. Asked why this should happen, Mattson replied, 'If you think of it in evolutionary terms it makes sense. If you are hungry you better increase your cognitive ability. It will give you a survival advantage if you can remember the location of the food.'

This documentary was looking at the health benefits of fasting, and certainly the evidence suggested that occasional fasting might be good for you — not only with weight loss and other health benefits but also for brain function. It also has far wider implications, however. Mattson is now conducting human trials to test if the same phenomenon occurs in human beings, but it's highly likely that it does. We already know that the brain can and does change itself depending on the environment — it's known as *neuroplasticity*.

If hunger stresses the brain matter in the same way that exercise stresses the muscles, then hunger really does make the brain sharper. Hunger is a physical crisis that forces the body out of complacency and comfort; it triggers action. It's highly likely, therefore, that a crisis of any sort that initiates a physical stress response will also trigger intense brain function. In short, we get more creative in a crisis. Why? Because we are fighting for survival!

In moments of crisis or severe adversity our mind and body will shift gear and often access resources that we simply didn't know existed prior to the event.

On 9 April 1982 Angela Cavallo's teenage son Tony was out in the yard tinkering under his beloved 1964 Chevy Impala. Without warning, the two jacks holding up the car slipped and the car fell, pinning Tony underneath. Hearing a loud noise, Angela went out to the yard to see what had happened and was horrified to find her son unconscious beneath the car. Angela, in her late fifties at the time, lifted the car and held it up for five full minutes while two neighbours replaced the jacks and pulled Tony to safety.

It's unlikely that Angela would ever have known her own capabilities had she not been in a crisis. Physiologists Michio Ikai and Arthur H. Steinhaus demonstrated that human strength could be increased by up to 31 per cent in certain situations, one being panic. In an article published in the *Journal of Applied Physiology*, they concluded that what we 'think' we are capable of is nothing more than a conditioned response or habit that limits our full potential. In other words, we are all capable of considerably more than we consistently demonstrate but it often takes a crisis for us to shift gears and effectively tap into that capacity.

Considered from this vantage point, it's easy to see crisis as a potential blessing. Sometimes severe adversity is simply the universe's way of telling you that you are on the wrong path and need to make some changes. Crisis is good for you! Without crisis it is so easy to drown in mediocrity — a no-man's-land where the status quo is not bad enough to change but isn't very good either. Crisis forces our hand. It demands change while also giving you fast-track access to resources such as creativity, innovation and strength that you probably didn't know you had.

Obviously crisis situations are not easy to handle. They can be extremely stressful and too much stress, especially over a long period of time, can adversely affect our health.

In periods of panic, for example, the body will move into fight- or-flight mode for self-preservation. All the blood will be pushed into the extremities, the limbs, ready for action — as illustrated by Angela Cavallo! Brain function can also be inhibited as the neocortex, the thinking part of your brain, effectively shuts down. When you find yourself in a stressful situation your limbic system, the emotional centre of your brain, will kick into gear and move you into action long before the message of danger has even reached the thinking part of your brain, the neocortex. In his groundbreaking book *Emotional Intelligence*, Daniel Goldman explains how Joseph LeDoux, a neuroscientist at the Center for Neural Science at New York University, was the first to discover the important function of the amygdala. These two almond-shaped clusters of interconnected cells that sit above the brain stem, one in each hemisphere, essentially act as our 'emotional sentinel'. Goldman tells the story of a friend of his in England who, having eaten lunch at a canal-side café, took a stroll along the canal. After a few minutes he saw a girl gazing into the water, her face frozen in fear. Before he knew it Goldman's friend was in the water. Only once in the water did he realise why — and he was able to save a toddler who had fallen in.

It was his amygdala that caused him to jump in the canal. Our brain is switched 'on' all the time; it processes all the information it receives from the five senses and makes decisions on the basis of that data. It had always been thought that the neocortex, or the conscious thinking brain, receives the information first and sends out signals to the respective parts of the brain for action. What LeDoux discovered was that the amygdala gets the information first and is effectively able to hijack the brain and initiate a reaction, often before the thinking brain even knows what's going on. Goldman's friend picked up a danger signal from the face of the girl looking at the water and reacted immediately by jumping into the water. It was only once he was in the water that his neocortex got with the program and he could understand why he had done it.

So while a crisis or challenging situation can sharpen the mind, if the body feels stressed over a long period this can backfire. The solution, therefore, is to engage the thinking brain as quickly as possible and get into action.

This idea of increased brain activity and function also ties into learning. For years scientists thought the brain was hardwired. It was assumed that whatever brain cells we were born with were our lot and when some died they were not replaced. In the 1980s it was discovered that we could generate new brain cells in response to certain demands. As we've seen, one of those demands is physical hunger. Another is learning, and again this is related to the neuroplasticity of the brain during crisis.

Neurons or brain cells are created or regenerated in response to a new learning challenge. When we are faced with a crisis of any type, the situation usually demands that we adapt and learn new ways of thinking and working in order to navigate the crisis effectively. Being challenged is therefore an important part of growth and development. We literally think differently when challenged and stressed. It appears that brain function responds favourably to demands and actually performs better in a crisis or difficulty, all of which makes sense from an evolutionary perspective. Your brain needs to be stretched and challenged. Sharp, clear and innovative thinking is therefore more readily available when push really comes to shove. It would appear that when we *really* need to find a solution, the brain will adapt and help us find one.

At least, it will if you foster the habits that determine whether you will be able to turn crisis into opportunity.

## Habits: Crisis creates opportunity

When crisis hits or you find yourself in a difficult or challenging situation, there are certain things you need to do and actions you need to take consistently if you want to emerge stronger from the experience. In short, you need to foster the following habits:

1. Connect to your why.
2. Think impossible thoughts.
3. Direct your focus.
4. Create another crisis.

### 1 CONNECT TO YOUR WHY

As I mentioned in the introduction, I genuinely believe my accident was a blessing for me because it forced me to realign my purpose by looking at my life and what was *really* important. I got my half-time opportunity long before mid life and I consider myself extremely fortunate for that alone. Crisis is tough. It can be traumatic and extremely painful emotionally, physically and financially, but when viewed from a new vantage point crisis is one of the most powerful and effective initiators of change because it allows us to connect or reconnect to our purpose.

One of my favourite books is *Start with Why: How Great Leaders Inspire Everyone to Take Action* by Simon Sinek. Sinek opens by telling the story of Samuel Pierpont Langley and how he set out to be the first man to pilot an airplane at the start of the twentieth century. Langley was a highly regarded mathematician, astronomer, physicist, inventor and aviation pioneer. He had influential and powerful friends, including Andrew Carnegie and Alexander Graham Bell. And he had money: based on the success of his previous aviation models, Langley was awarded a $50 000 grant from the War Department and a $20 000 grant from the Smithsonian Institute, where he was also a senior officer.

In today's money that's about $1.8 million, so it was a significant level of funding with which to pursue his dream. It allowed him to attract a 'dream team of talent and know-how'. They had access to the finest materials and equipment and the press followed their every move. Langley had everything he needed to secure success.

Several hundred miles away in Dayton, Ohio, two guys you may be more familiar with — Wilbur and Orville Wright — were working in a bicycle shop on the same dream. The Wright brothers didn't have powerful friends or university degrees or distinguished careers, and they didn't have access to funding or materials. In fact, no-one on their team had so much as a college degree — not even the brothers themselves. Working in a cramped shop with a small group of equally committed and passionate aviation nuts drawn together from the local area, on 17 December 1903 Wilbur and Orville Wright became the first to make a controlled, powered human flight.

So what happened in this David and Goliath battle? Langley had everything: he was smart, he was educated, he was cashed up and he had powerful connections. What he didn't have, however, was a big enough *why*. Wilbur and Orville Wright had none of the obvious advantages that Langley enjoyed, but they had something far more valuable: they were obsessed with flight, it was their passion and that gave them a compelling why.

Sinek writes of how the founders of Apple were not motivated by money. Considering the price of Apple products today compared with its competitors it's a little hard to credit, but Steve Jobs and Steve Wozniak believed that technology was not just for business. They saw the personal computer as 'a way for the little man to take on a corporation'. They wanted to create simple, beautiful and elegant technology that made life better, easier and more fun. And by starting with the right *why* they were able to revolutionise the industry despite being the underdog for many years.

Sinek goes on to tell us about the Golden Circle model, which introduces the three key words *what, how* and *why*. We all know 'what' we do each and every day: what work we are in, what services we provide, and what products we offer. Many know 'how' we do the what, so we know how we create the results we do, our differentiating value proposition, our uniqueness. Yet few of us can answer 'why' we do what we do. Why do we get out of bed each morning? Why are we involved in this business and not that one? Why have we chosen to work in one profession instead of another, and why should anyone care?

When you have a strong 'why', the 'how' becomes almost secondary. When the goal is important enough, people will surmount all types of obstacles and endure all sorts of hardship to achieve that outcome.

One man who stands out in this regard is Viktor Frankl. Frankl was a respected Austrian neurologist and psychiatrist when the Second World War began. As a Jew he was first ordered to stop treating 'Aryan' patients. On 25 September 1942 he and his wife and parents were deported to the Nazi Theresienstadt Ghetto. On 19 October 1944 Frankl and his wife were transported to the Auschwitz concentration camp.

Before this Frankl had finished writing his life's work and, desperate to keep it safe, had sewn it into the lining of his coat. In an interview when he was 90 years old Frankl told how he had begged the guards who discovered it, 'Look, this is the manuscript of a scientific book . . . I must keep this manuscript at all costs; it contains my life's work. Do you understand that?' They simply mocked him and the manuscript was destroyed. Frankl recalled, 'At that moment I saw the plain truth and did what marked the culminating point of the first phase of my psychological reaction: I struck out my whole former life.'

What followed was unspeakable horror. His wife died in the Bergen-Belsen concentration camp; his mother was killed in the gas chambers of Auschwitz; his brother also died at Auschwitz. Apart from Frankl himself the only other member of his family to survive the Holocaust was his sister, who escaped from Austria and emigrated to Australia.

What makes Frankl unique is that he was able to live out his own theory. He used his own ideas to find meaning in utter hopelessness. He became obsessed with his why, which was to survive so he could share his insights with the world. Desperate to re-create the book he had lost, he wrote on every scrap of paper he could find. After he was eventually liberated by the Americans in 1945 he went on to write a little book called *Man's Search for Meaning* and to develop his theories of logotherapy and existential therapy, which have helped millions of people to find meaning in their own lives, regardless of the darkness they may face.

Without that why, having lost almost all of his family and his life's work, and experiencing the daily atrocities of the Nazi concentration camps, it would have been easy to give up. But as Frankl said, 'Between stimulus and response, there is a space. In that space is our power to choose our response. In our response lies our growth and our freedom.' There may have been nothing he could do about his external circumstances, but the Nazis could not control his internal condition, and that final freedom saved his life.

Without that why, there is nothing to pull someone through difficult times, so they quit at the first sign of trouble. Having a goal is one thing; having the courage to pursue it once things get difficult is quite another. And having a strong enough why is the key. The great thing about crisis is that it can force you to think about your why. As a result, it offers unprecedented opportunity to re-create and revolutionise your life moving forward.

For most of us life just happens. Chances are you didn't sit down one day to map out your life plan. You didn't decide how old you'd be when you got married or when you would have children or what profession you would enter. Often these big life choices just happen as a result of circumstances.

In my training programs I often ask the audience, 'How many people in this room spend more time planning their holiday than they do planning their lives?' I've found that more than 90 per cent of the thousands of people I've spoken to around the world spend more time planning their holiday than planning their lives. This highlights two issues: first, that our education systems have not taught us the importance of consistent life planning and, second, that we lack the passion and drive for long-term personal life planning.

If you are like most people, when you left school or university you just took one of the first jobs you could find, and that accident of timing is what directed your fate more than any soul-searching that you may or may not have done. It's the same in business: once a business generates momentum, the leader becomes a firefighter rather than a strategist or tactician. The months melt into years and before you know where you are you are in a different market, providing a different service and wondering how you got there.

Crisis can be a fantastic opportunity to jam on the brakes and really assess what is happening and match that back to your own hopes and dreams. And often those hopes and dreams have become so obscured by day-to-day life and work that it can take a little while to reconnect.

That was certainly true for me. I thought I was happy with life. I was super busy, I had a job I loved and I had a lot of freedom in that role, which I enjoyed even more. I also had my own studio, a beautiful wife and two gorgeous daughters. But I can't say I ever really planned all that. It had just evolved that way, and although I was exhausted and I didn't see much of my family I thought I was successful.

Then I had my accident and everything changed. As I lay dying in the smashed-up Holden my mind was racing. It felt like my life was on fast-forward on an old videotape — I got glimpses of what was being covered and I knew it all made sense, but I couldn't make everything out. As I said earlier, I was aware of my entire life up to that point, how one thing led to another and how connected everything was. Then suddenly the tape stopped and three questions came into clear focus:

» Was I PASSIONATE?

» Was I PRODUCTIVE?

» Was I MAKING A DIFFERENCE?

I remember feeling totally lost and utterly alone, despite knowing that there was a crowd of people around me willing me to survive. I didn't realise it at the time but I was coming face to face with my why.

The weird thing about a question is that once it's asked your brain, even a bleeding and bruised one, has to answer. So I remember struggling to think about the questions. Was I passionate about life, about business, about my family, my job, my work colleagues and about the things that I said mattered to me? Was I productive in my life, toward my family, my parents, in my team, in my dreams, my social community, to others less fortunate than me? And was I making a difference to my family and friends, to my neighbourhood, to the wider community, to humanity?

I knew in my heart that the answer wasn't always what I wanted or hoped it would be. Before the accident I was always rushing from place to place. It was the life I'd wanted, and although I was enjoying most of it I knew I was failing in the most important area. I remembered a night a few months earlier when I arrived home late, again. I'd been away most of the week and a client was waiting for me in my home studio. As I rushed in the door I went straight to my study, getting ready to apologise to the client. Emelia ran up to me and squealed, 'Daddy, Daddy, you're home.' I just brushed her off: 'Look out Milly, out of the way, I'm late.' I still get choked up thinking how I dismissed her.

My crisis forced me to connect to my why. I wasn't interested in scaling some corporate ladder or graduating to a bigger and better house. I wanted a life of meaning and experiences that put my family at the heart of my life, not the periphery. I wanted to spend the second half of my life being passionate, caring and making a difference to others.

Just by seeing crisis differently you can shift the meaning from nightmare to blessing. Take Al Gore as another example. You might imagine that Gore's why was political — to effect political change through government. After all, he rose to the office of US Vice President in 1993. By that point Gore had been in politics since 1977 and in 2000 he ran for president against George W. Bush. But then a crisis hit and the election ended up being one of the most controversial in recent history. Although Gore won the popular vote by some 500 000 votes, he lost the Electoral College when the US Supreme Court stepped in over the Florida vote recount and ruled 5–4 in favour of Bush.

Gore had failed to achieve his goal. I can only imagine how devastated he must have been. But what you might not know is that ever since his senior year at Harvard, when he took a class with oceanographer and global warming theorist Roger Revelle, Gore had been fascinated by environmental issues including climate change. His 'failure' in the presidential campaign had forced Gore to reconnect to his real passion, motivation and why. He probably thought the best way to effect change in the environment was through government legislation, but Al Gore's contribution to environmental issues may have been considerably greater since his exit from politics.

Gore didn't leave politics a bitter, angry man, even though he had every right to following the scandalous injustice of the 2000 vote. Instead he reconnected to his why and went on to create the game-changing documentary *An Inconvenient Truth*. And he has probably done more to further the environmental cause since leaving politics than he could ever have achieved as president. Al Gore even won the Nobel Peace Prize for his climate change activism.

Everyone has a different why, but in my experience it rarely revolves around money or making a profit. Money is an outcome; in itself it has no meaning or purpose. Most people want to be financially comfortable but meaning, experience and using their talents and abilities are much more important. The problem is we can become so focused on paying bills, meeting sales targets and attending endless meetings that we lose sight of the things that really make us happy and fulfilled.

Crisis is the universe's way of calling time on the status quo so you can work out what it is you really want. It gives you the opportunity to bounce forward into not just any future so you find yourself in another crisis down the track, but *that* future. You can't hit a target you don't know you have!

## Start bouncing

### The car crash test

Although this may sound a little morbid, take a moment to imagine that tomorrow you jump in your car and on the way to your destination you are involved in an accident. You can hear the sirens approaching and you have a few moments to review your life.

You don't understand what happened and you're not 100 per cent sure you are going to be okay. What do you think about first? Who shows up in your thoughts? What do you most regret not doing? What do you regret doing? What makes you smile? What makes you cringe?

If, by a miracle, fate allows you another chance, what would you change? Write down five things you would change and why.

## Start bouncing

### The Felix Felicis test

In *Harry Potter and the Half-Blood Prince* Harry wins a small vial of Felix Felicis in his potions class at Hogwarts.

Felix Felicis is 'liquid luck' and whoever drinks it is guaranteed success in whatever they attempt. Imagine you had a permanent supply of Felix Felicis so whatever you do you cannot fail. What would you do with the rest of your life?

## 2 THINK IMPOSSIBLE THOUGHTS

Albert Einstein famously said, 'The significant problems we face cannot be solved at the same level of thinking we were at when we created them.' This is pretty logical and yet often when we find ourselves in crisis we attempt to find a solution using the same information and thinking that got us into the crisis in the first place. The same thinking leads us to bounce back to the place we were before the crisis happened.

It doesn't work. We need to start fresh, wipe the slate clean and begin to think impossible thoughts, and this won't necessarily happen naturally. William James, one of the most original thinkers in history, said, 'A great many people think they are thinking when they are merely rearranging their prejudices.' In other words, what we consider thinking is nothing more than moving around the same ideas and thoughts we've already had. We need to upload new information and deliberately seek new ideas and possibilities. Only then can we activate the full potential of our brain, unlock innovative solutions to curly questions and bounce forward.

For decades personal development literature has discussed the power of thought, but it's only relatively recently that scientific research has backed up the idea. Physicist and pioneer in psychoenergetic research Dr William Tiller of Stanford University has conducted many studies that have demonstrated just how much intention and thought influence outcome.

In one of his most widely cited studies Tiller had four skilled meditators focus on an electrical device to 'imprint' it with a specific intention — to increase the pH by one unit. These devices, together with control devices, were then placed six inches from separate samples of water taken from the same source. To clarify the significance of this increase, if you were to increase the pH in the human body by one unit it would be fatal. Statistically the chances of it happening accidentally or naturally are less than one in a thousand. However, the boxes that had focused mental energy directed toward them did indeed alter the pH of the water.

In his book *Hidden Messages in Water*, Dr Masaru Emoto also demonstrates the power of thought to influence outcome. In a series of experiments Emoto took 50 samples of water from the same source and froze them for three hours. At −5° C the frozen crystals were photographed through a microscope. The experiment was then repeated using the same water, only this time the water had been exposed to various stimuli such as music, words and prayer. What he discovered was that music by Beethoven, prayer and words such as 'love' and 'thank you' taped to the sample produced beautiful, intricate and perfectly symmetrical crystals. Heavy metal music and phrases such as 'You make me sick, I will kill you' created incomplete, distorted and malformed crystals.

We can sense the energy of others or the 'energy in a room'. On a really basic level we already know that it feels better being around positive, happy people than being around negative, unhappy people. So while Dr Emoto's research is highly controversial and dismissed by some as pseudoscience, it points to something we already instinctively know — that energy matters. And considering that what we think about affects energy, then his findings are not that surprising after all. This is why it's so important to consciously direct your focus and take charge of your thinking, especially during difficult times. If all your energy is directed toward what you don't want to happen, then, these studies imply, you could actually be bringing about the outcome you desperately want to avoid by focusing on the negative as opposed to the positive.

As a result of his own research Tiller concluded, 'From these studies and more like them, it can be seen that belief fuels expectations and expectations, in turn, marshal intention at both unconscious and conscious levels to fulfil expectations.' According to Tiller, 'We are running the holodeck. It has such flexibility that anything you can imagine, it will create for you. Your intention causes this thing to materialize once you're conscious enough and you learn how to use your intentionality.'

For those readers not familiar with *Star Trek*, Tiller's reference to the holodeck is from *Star Trek: The Next Generation*. Like the crew of the USS *Enterprise*, who could enter the holodeck and dial up any simulated alternative reality either to assist with training or to relax from the rigours of space travel, we use our thoughts — consciously or unconsciously — to dial up our own reality based on what we choose to focus our intention and habitual thinking on.

Tiller is by no means alone in his thinking. Philosopher and theologian Dr Micheál Ledwith puts it this way: 'Reality is not solid, it's mostly empty space and whatever solidity it has seems more to resemble a hologram picture rather than solid harsh reality. It's a shimmering reality that seems to be very susceptible to the power of thought.' Interestingly, Ledwith was ordained as a Catholic priest in 1967. He was appointed a lecturer in theology at the Pontifical University, Maynooth, in 1971, becoming professor, then dean of faculty, vice president and finally president. From 1980 to 1997 he also served three terms as a member of the International Theological Commission, a small group of theologians who advise on matters referred to them by the Pope. Ledwith suggests:

> We are creating our own reality every day, though we find that very hard to accept— there's nothing more exquisitely pleasant than to blame somebody else for the way we are. It's her fault or it's his fault; it's the system; it's God; it's my parents . . . Whatever way we observe the world around us is what comes back to us, and for that reason why my life for instance is so lacking in joy and happiness and fulfilment is because my focus is lacking in those same things exactly.

There is now irrefutable proof that what we think about on a habitual basis influences what we experience. If we expect the worst, then we can't really be very surprised when it comes about.

It follows that Einstein was right: whatever thinking brought about the problem will not be good enough to solve it.

In my own life I have experienced many traumas and adversities, yet none was as great as my accident in 2006. The doctors, nurses, occupational therapists and physiotherapist were 'beyond impressed' at my remarkable rehabilitation and healing following my accident. One doctor even told a newspaper that my recovery was nothing short of miraculous. Many people go through horrific trauma, some greater than mine. But why did I overcome my adversity physically, emotionally and mentally faster and better than most other people? I believe that part of the answer is because I was thinking impossible thoughts. I was constantly focused on the positive daily, weekly and monthly results I was aiming for through my recovery stages. My thoughts strongly contributed to my rehabilitation mentally, emotionally and physically, and I would even go as far as to say spiritually and financially too.

It has also been proven that thought alters the biological make- up of the body and can change the neural networks of the brain. In one study published in the *Journal of Neurophysiology* in 1995, four groups of volunteers were monitored to assess how well they improved their ability to play the piano. The first group were told to memorise a specific one-hand, five-finger sequence, which they had to physically practise for two hours on a piano every day for five days. The second group were told to play the piano for two hours without any instruction over the course of the same five days. The third group never touched a piano but were given the opportunity to observe what was taught to the first group, until they had memorised it. Then they were told to mentally rehearse the same sequence for two hours every day for five days. So they didn't actually play a piano but they *imagined* themselves playing the piano. The final group was the control group, who didn't do anything related to the piano.

Once the five days were complete the researchers used a technique called *transcranial magnetic stimulation* to measure any brain changes that had taken place. What was surprising was that the group who had not played the piano but imagined themselves going through the same routine as the group who actually played the piano showed almost exactly the same neural expansion and development in exactly the same specific area of their brain. And this group showed greater proficiency than the group who did actually play the piano but played whatever they liked!

By now I hope you recognise that what you think about and how you direct your focus will have a profound effect on your results. Get creative, turn your thinking upside down and think impossible thoughts and you are much more likely to find innovative solutions to difficult situations.

**NECESSITY IS THE MOTHER OF INVENTION.**
**– ENGLISH PROVERB**

When we need something — say, to achieve a goal or solve a problem — and that objective becomes imperative, then we are often forced to find a way.

By the 18th century Niagara Falls was becoming a popular tourist spot and pressure was mounting to build a bridge to support tourism and trade between Canada on one side and the United States on the other.

In 1847 an innovative civil engineer, Charles Ellet Jr, was commissioned to build a bridge across the narrowest point of the falls above the beginning of the Whirlpool Rapids. Most bridge builders and the general public thought the idea was crazy and didn't believe that a suspension bridge was even possible. The narrowest point the bridge needed to span was 800 feet and the first problem was how to get a line across the water. It was far too dangerous to cross the falls by boat. Airplanes had not yet been invented and 800 feet was far too far for even the best bowshot. Ellet could not build the bridge if he could not first connect the two sides in some way. Necessity being the mother of invention, he decided to hold a kite-flying contest. The first person to fly their kite across the Niagara Gorge would win $5 (equivalent to $120 today). It would have been quite an incentive for the local kids.

The winner was a young American boy named Homan Walsh, who successfully completed the task from the Canadian shoreline. A light string was attached to his kite, and it was then fastened to a tree on the US side and used to pull across progressively heavier string, cord, rope and finally wire cable. A similar technique is still used to moor large ships. Often the mooring lines used to secure the vessel are far too heavy and awkward to throw from the ship to the quay. To solve this problem light 'heaving lines', attached to the mooring lines, are thrown to the quay first. The heavier mooring lines can then be hauled across to secure the ship.

Ellet attached the heaving line to Homan Walsh's kite, and it worked! The first Niagara Falls Suspension Bridge was completed on 26 July 1848.

Sir James Dyson, the British industrial designer who founded the Dyson Company after creating the first bagless vacuum cleaner, is a classic example of what can be achieved when you think impossible thoughts. Until Dyson, manufacturers had no incentive to create a bagless vacuum cleaner because the bags provided them with an additional revenue stream. But Dyson believed there was a better way and set out on what he called 'purposeful failures', in which he deliberately set out to try things that conventional wisdom said wouldn't work. Dyson says, 'It was wrong-doing rather than wrong-thinking. That's not easy, because we're all taught to do things the right way.'

After he'd exhausted all the probable solutions he turned to all the improbable solutions, eventually experimenting with a shape that was the opposite of what he thought would work. It took Dyson many years and 5127 prototypes before he cracked it, but his Dyson Dual Cyclone vacuum cleaner revolutionised the industry and today Sir James Dyson is a billionaire. Not a bad result for 'wrong-doing'.

While researching this section of the book I discovered that in 1876 Maria Spelterini became the only woman ever to cross the Niagara Gorge on a tightrope. At the age of just 23 she made four separate crossings within weeks of each other. On 8 July she crossed using a 5.7-cm wire. Four days later she crossed the same wire with wooden peach baskets strapped to her feet! A week after that she crossed again, only this time she was blindfolded. Finally, before retiring from Niagara, she made the crossing with her ankles and wrists handcuffed. Gives you a whole new perspective on impossible, doesn't it!

## Start bouncing

### Mission impossible

Take a moment to think of a problem or difficulty you are currently experiencing. It could be a personal problem or a business challenge. Imagine an eccentric millionaire is offering a $100 000 reward for the worst solution to your problem. Don't think too hard about this but write down 10 of the worst, most outlandish, crazy ideas you can think of as possible solutions to the problem. Deliberately write down things that feel wrong or are the opposite of the solutions already playing around in your head.

## 3  DIRECT YOUR FOCUS

Our experience of reality, our interpretation of a crisis or challenging situation, depends largely on what we decide the situation means. And often that decision comes down to what we choose to focus on.

Ever since my accident in 2006 I have experienced something called 'phantom pain'. This means I feel pain in my right arm even though I no longer have a right arm. When I close my eyes I can still feel my fingers, my wrist and my elbow as though they're still there. My right elbow was 'alienated' in the accident, which meant my hand was only just attached to what remained of my right arm. When the doctors realised they couldn't rebuild it, while I was in a coma they asked my wife for permission to amputate. Today I live with an above-elbow amputation of my right arm.

It wasn't an easy decision for Kate to make, especially given that it was my right arm. I was right-handed and she knew it would be difficult for me to adjust. I used to love playing guitar too. She worried that I would resent her for making the decision.

Of course I never did. What's interesting looking back is that Kate had already started to consciously direct her focus as a way to navigate the stress *she* was under. Kate had always been taught the value of trying to find a positive in even the worst situations, so when the doctor was waiting for her response she was busy searching her mind for a positive spin on the surgery. After a few moments she looked up at the doctor, smiled and said, 'Well . . . at least he can still wear his wedding ring!'

She laughs about it now because the doctor looked at her as though she was nuts, but Kate gave her consent and the surgery took place. And once I woke up it became pretty clear to me that I was going to have to start consciously directing my focus too.

Even today, years later, I am often woken up in the night by the phantom pain. To give you an idea of what the pain feels like, imagine that you have been leaning against your arm for hours until you get those really stabbing pins and needles. Normally when you get that sensation you can stretch out your arm to get the blood circulating again and the feeling subsides. Obviously I don't have recourse to that solution so it just gets more and more intense. If you imagine the worst pins and needles you've ever had and multiply that by 100 — that's what I experience in my right arm 24/7.

Phantom pain is a common phenomenon among people who have lost a limb through amputation or injury, and unfortunately there is little in the way of cure or treatment. In 2012 I had the most amazing privilege of meeting and speaking on the same stage as Dr V. S. Ramachandran, a neuroscientist known for his work in the fields of behavioural neurology and phantom psychophysics. He is director of the Center for Brain and Cognition and currently a professor in the Department of Psychology at the University of California, San Diego. Dr Ramachandran has theorised that there is a link between the phenomenon of phantom limbs and neural plasticity in the adult human brain. He believes that neuroimaging can reduce the sensation of phantom pain. To this end he invented the mirror box and mirror visual feedback as a treatment for conditions associated with phantom limb pain, stroke and regional pain syndrome.

As the first scientist to emphasise the role of cortical reorganisation as the basis for phantom limb sensations, Ramachandran is often referred to as 'the Marco Polo of neuroscience'. His contribution to neuroscience has been considerable and in 2011 *Time* magazine listed him as one of 'the most influential people in the world'.

After thinking about my conversations with Ramachandran and using his mirror box technique with little result, I've concentrated on conditioning myself to use the phantom pain as a reminder to consciously direct my focus elsewhere. Today, if I bruise myself I can consciously shift my focus to my amputated arm and the pain of the new injury will basically disappear. So I've conditioned myself not to experience the pain. It is something we can all do just by gaining control over our thinking. I do this through a formula I like to call *cognitive disassociation*.

Cognitive disassociation is a process by which you deflect your thoughts and energy elsewhere. It's like rerouting your focus. If you experience pain or discomfort, you can neurologically shift your focus onto something else. You've probably experienced this process yourself. Perhaps you felt queasy and just as you were beginning to focus on this feeling something distracted you — maybe you got an urgent phone call or you were called into a meeting. Ten minutes later you'll remember you felt sick and realise the feeling disappeared. All parents are very familiar with the distraction technique!

Below are the five steps that can help you to embrace cognitive disassociation in your own life — personally or professionally.

1. Consciously disrupt your focus. The quickest and easiest way to do this is to change your physiology. So do something different and physically move your body — go for a walk or run, or just put on your favourite track and dance about for a few minutes!

2. Purposely create a new state that is pleasurable and appealing. Initially you may have to force this new state or pretend you feel confident or excited, but persevere and it will become second nature.

3. Stay stimulated in your new state. Find ways to stay connected and motivated in this new state.

4. Anticipate uncertainty. Constant stimulation is key as it keeps engagement levels high, so stay busy and in motion.

5. Create a new state. The faster the pace, the more distraction from the initial pain you will experience.

Russian physiologist Ivan Pavlov is famous for uncovering the process of conditioning. What Pavlov discovered was that if he fed his dogs while also ringing a bell for long enough, the dog would come to associate the sound of the bell with food. After a relatively short period of time all Pavlov needed to do was ring the bell and his dogs would start to salivate. He called this discovery a *conditioned reflex,* and it's since been discovered that human beings learn in much the same way.

What few people realise is that thought and feeling are connected by a two-way loop. If you think you are depressed, you will begin to create the internal chemical signature of depression and you will feel depressed. Depression has a particular chemical composition, as do all emotions. Alternatively, the body can create this chemical composition and you can start to think you're depressed. Thoughts and feelings are therefore a two-way system. Or, as cancer pioneer Carl Simonton puts it, 'Mind, body and emotions are a unitary system — affect one and you affect the others.'

This means you can pretend you don't feel the pain or you can pretend you are confident or excited or positive, and the brain will activate the internal chemical cocktail maker, which will produce the recipe for confident, excited or positive so you will begin actually to feel confident, excited or positive. This may sound a little delusional, but pretending you have certain feelings or character traits is not like pretending you can play the violin or speak five languages — those things are skills that must be learned and practised.

I can't change my phantom pain; it is something I am probably going to have to live with for the rest of my life. But I can change the way I think about it and I can change what it means; I can tone down the pain so I just don't notice it. You have considerably more control over what you think and how you feel than you perhaps currently realise. And if you can master your internal landscape, then you can master anything.

**IF YOU ARE PAINED BY EXTERNAL THINGS, IT IS NOT THEY THAT DISTURB YOU, BUT YOUR JUDGEMENT OF THEM. AND IT IS IN YOUR POWER TO WIPE OUT THAT JUDGEMENT NOW.**
**– MARCUS AURELIUS**

How you see the world and how I see the world are different. I know that for sure because I have a different background from you. I am one of 11 children, brought up on a farm in Tasmania,

Australia, with an Indian mother and a Scottish father. That upbringing, which was very much focused around religion, has influenced my life profoundly. As a result of that upbringing, the people I've met and the experiences I've had, I have a set of beliefs and values that influence how I view the world.

You also have a set of values and beliefs that influence how you see the world. You and I interpret the vast amount of information that is available through our five senses, which in turn is filtered through our beliefs and values, and that's how we make sense of the world. Interestingly, one of the really quirky consequences of my accident was that all my senses were heightened. I asked my doctors about this and they explained that because the right side of my body had been so badly damaged my brain began to compensate by increasing the access to data from my senses of sight, sound, taste, touch and smell.

Of course, the different influx of data we each experience means that 'reality' is not objective. Your version of reality and mine are likely to be quite different. If you doubt that, ask a policeman how different witness statements can be at the scene of a crime. Ten people could see the same event and each one would remember it differently. Witness one might have noticed the time because she had just received a phone call from her mother telling her that her favourite TV show was about to start. Witness two noticed what the perpetrator was wearing because his brother has the same jacket. Witness eight might have seen something completely different based on their particular experience.

So everyone experiences the world slightly differently based on their own filter system, which involves their beliefs, attitudes, values, experiences and so on. This means that in any given moment we are interpreting and adding meaning to the information available to us through our five senses. We think we make objective, rational decisions because we are aware of all there is to be aware of, but we are not.

According to author and psychology professor Mihaly Csikszentmihalyi (pronounced *cheeks-sent-me-hi*), our capacity to process information accurately is actually very limited. In his book *Flow: The Psychology of Happiness: The Classic Work on How to Achieve Happiness,* he argues:

> At this point in our scientific knowledge we are on the verge of being able to estimate how much information the central nervous system is capable of processing. It seems that we can manage at most 7 bits of information— such as differentiated sounds, or visual stimuli, or recognizable nuances of emotion or thought— at any one time, and that the shortest time it takes to discriminate between one set of bits and another is about 1/18th of a second. By using these figures one concludes that it is possible to process at most 126 bits of information per second.

That's actually not so much considering that it has been estimated that we are privy to around 2000 000 bits of information per second. If we were to become consciously aware of all that data we would go insane, so the brain filters it. In his book *The Doors of Perception,* Aldous Huxley refers to this brain function as a 'reducing valve' that ensures only a tiny, manageable proportion of information makes it through to conscious awareness.

In effect, your brain is like a newspaper editor; it assesses all the data or stories 'behind the scenes' then decides what headline to release to your awareness based on its relative importance in your life. Or, as Csikszentmihalyi puts it, 'An individual can experience only so much. Therefore, the information we allow into consciousness becomes extremely important; it is, in fact, what determines the content and quality of life.' What you focus on will shape your life and will help you to bounce forward. And unless you consciously direct that focus, the content and quality of your life will be left to chance.

One famous experiment that brilliantly demonstrates the implications of focus was conducted by Dr Daniel Simons of the University of Illinois and Christopher Chabris of Harvard University. In this study university students were asked to watch a short video of two teams playing basketball. They were told to focus on one team in particular and to record the number of passes made between the players in that team.

Halfway through the game a woman in a gorilla suit walked onto the basketball court and wandered through the players for a full seven seconds. At one point the 'gorilla' even turned to face the camera and beat its chest! When reporting back their answers and providing feedback on the experiment, half the participants hadn't even seen the gorilla. In fact, many were so irate over the claim that they could have missed something so obvious that they insisted on seeing the video again. They had been so focused on counting the passes between the players that they had missed the gorilla altogether. What could we be missing when we are totally wrapped up in a crisis? What opportunities have we ignored already?

In another experiment organised by the *Washington Post*, a young man entered a Washington DC subway station just before 8 am on Friday, 12 January 2007. He took position against a wall and started to play his violin. He played six pieces of music by the composer Bach and played for a total of 43 minutes. During that time 1097 people passed him, most on their way to work. Only seven people stopped to listen — even for a minute or two. Twenty-seven people gave money, mostly on the run, and the busker collected the princely sum of $32.17. When he finished no-one noticed and there was no applause. They didn't listen because their focus was elsewhere, and because of that they missed a musical performance by Joshua Bell, one of the greatest musicians in the world, playing one of the most intricate pieces of music ever written. He was playing a 1713 handcrafted violin by Antonio Stradivari valued at $3.5 million. Three days before the experiment Joshua Bell had played to a sell-out audience at Boston's Symphony Hall, where his talents commanded a fee of about $1000 a minute, rather than $32 an hour.

If we can miss a gorilla on the basketball court and fail to notice one of the most brilliant musicians of our time playing in a subway station, isn't it fair to assume that we are missing opportunities and possibilities that could improve our life tenfold, just because we are not directing our focus properly? And if that is true on a normal day, is it not especially true in a crisis?

In times of crisis we tend to batten down the hatches. Our focus becomes even narrower and more rigid as we struggle to cope with the influx of additional information. In effect, we either narrow our focus so far that we can't see the wood for the trees or we expand it so wide that we are overwhelmed by the scale of the challenges. Neither response is productive.

It's important that we consciously take charge of our focus. Often we can be tempted to take action — any sort of action — in an effort to resolve a situation. But unless you have assessed the scale and nature of the crisis you face, you are probably wasting time and energy on details and decisions that make no measurable difference to the crisis just so you can comfort yourself that, 'well, at least I'm doing something'. Getting busy does not always mean being productive. Scattering your focus to the four winds is often as useless as narrowing it to a single obsession. You need to control your focus so you can actively direct it toward solutions and positivity and away from fear and negativity. It's not always easy but this habit can change your life.

One company I really love is Wikipedia. This online encyclopaedia has opened up a new world of information to all of us. It's made access to information incredibly easy, fast and surprisingly reliable. Founder Jimmy Wales, who graduated from the University of Alabama with a master's in finance, was inspired by his love of print encyclopaedias and his craving for knowledge. But it was not all smooth sailing — far from it. His first attempt at creating an online encyclopaedia, Nupedia, failed. Then Wales shifted his focus toward collaboration, and today Wikipedia is the world's most visited online resource for reference material and information, while 2012 was the last year *Encyclopaedia Britannica* was in print.

Here's another example of the power of focus. When the director and the producer of a theatre production I was involved in both ditched, the project descended into crisis. After a vote from the cast, I was asked to direct, produce and choreograph the production. I had little experience in theatre at the time, but after seven months and directed focus and determination we managed to pull off a very successful sell-out show.

Consciously direct your focus to find some good from every situation. And if that's too hard initially, then direct your focus to the other good things in your life. This can often remind you that things are not all bad. Do you have two arms and two legs? Well, that's a start — you're already one up on me! Do you still have a roof over your head? Do your family and friends still love you? Now when I experience a particularly painful episode of phantom pain I use the pain to remind me how lucky I am.

Remember, the content and quality of your life do not depend on events or circumstances; they depend on you and what you choose to focus on. Will you focus on the problem or the solution? Will you focus on the past or the future? Will you focus on the positive or the negative?

Think of your crisis like an advanced driving lesson. The biggest reason people crash when they get into difficulties is that they panic and all their focus is directed toward the thing they don't want to hit. You're driving at speed heading into a corner and your instructor is telling you to look past the corner to where you want to go, but all you can see is the corner — and sure enough you crash into that corner. Crisis is the same. Often you're moving at speed toward a brick wall. You can focus either on the wall or what's past the wall. If you focus on the wall you *will* hit the wall. If you drag your focus away from the wall to the place you want to be, then you massively increase your chances of successfully manoeuvring past the obstacle. In the end we get what we focus on.

So if you find yourself in a pickle, if you've been made redundant or your business has gone into freefall and sales are drying up, dwelling on what went wrong isn't going to shift your focus. You need to break the cycle, expand your thinking and shift your focus in a new, positive direction. It may not be the right one, you may have to finetune it as you go along, but shift your focus and you will shift your results.

**THE HIGHEST STAGE IN MORAL CULTURE AT WHICH WE CAN ARRIVE IS WHEN WE RECOGNIZE THAT WE OUGHT TO CONTROL OUR THOUGHTS.**
**— CHARLES DARWIN**

## Start bouncing

### *Kate's game*

Take a moment to think of a problem or difficulty you are currently experiencing. It could be a personal problem or a business challenge. Write down a brief description of the issue. Now imagine that eccentric millionaire is back to offer you $100 000 for every positive perspective, idea or outcome you can come up with in relation to your current problem.

# 4 CREATE ANOTHER CRISIS

Even in the most turbulent life or business, crisis is not normally an everyday occurrence. Problems and challenges are.

We face problems all the time. Business challenges — cash flow, sales, people management, scheduling, meetings, new business, manufacturing, legal — are never ending. As a result, it's really easy to zone out from the constant pressure. Daily problems and frustrations can be annoying but are rarely enough to push you into action. There is no urgency to address these irritations. Problems tend not to demand the same attention as a good old-fashioned crisis. They can be ignored, deferred or forgotten. In fact, this procrastination is often the root cause of crisis. Most crises arise because a smaller, relatively inconsequential issue has been ignored for so long that it has become neither small nor inconsequential.

*Create another crisis* is about getting into the habit of escalating everything into a crisis so as to generate the types of creativity and innovation that only a crisis seems to initiate.

I first learned about this idea before my accident. I had been working in retail for a few years and had worked my way up to management level. I enjoyed it and it paid the bills — which was especially important when we discovered that Kate was expecting. After seven months she stopped work and I became the sole breadwinner, so I was acutely aware of the need to provide for my family.

I had picked up a solid business grounding in retail and at the time I was also involved in musical theatre, which really helped my confidence. But the hours were demanding and with a new member of the family on the way I wanted to secure a position that would give me a little more freedom. Sales seemed like the perfect solution, especially as I would be provided with a company car, mobile phone and laptop computer. So I applied for a position as a photocopier salesman. The role was very autonomous, which I loved as I could manage my hours around Kate and my baby daughter, although I have to admit it was hard motivating myself every day and the first six months were really tough. I think I sold one photocopier!

In time I got better and my improvement was definitely encouraged by the news that Kate was expecting our second child. The knowledge that soon there would be another little mouth to feed fuelled my determination and I managed to outperform many of the other leading photocopier brands. I was making good money. My performance had obviously caught the attention of the number one photocopier company, Xerox, who headhunted me for a new position and we were relocated to Launceston in northern Tasmania.

I didn't know many people in Launceston and I didn't have a network to tap into, so it took months to build up a client database. The job was a disaster and after a few short months I was fired because of a miscommunication, mainly by me. I was in crisis mode. I didn't really enjoy selling photocopiers, but I needed the money and I had a family that relied on me. The reality of my situation soon kicked in and I worked my tail off to secure something new. Looking back it was this financial crisis that forced me into creating a better life. And I remembered that experience when I was laid up in hospital after my accident.

**OPPORTUNITY IS MISSED BY MOST PEOPLE BECAUSE IT IS DRESSED IN OVERALLS AND LOOKS LIKE WORK.**
**– THOMAS EDISON**

After my accident the sole focus of my rehabilitation team was on getting me back to the same job I'd been doing at the time of the crash. But my body was very different. I was different — not just physically but mentally, emotionally and spiritually too.

I wasn't content going back to the same job. I had reconnected to my why — whether I'd wanted to or not — and my old life was no longer the life I wanted. It wasn't stimulating me and I felt there was something bigger and better out there with my name on it. I was frustrated by everyone around me who seemed hell- bent on getting me back to where I had been. I knew they were trying to help me, and I'll be eternally grateful to them for their perseverance and care during my rehabilitation, but it irritated me that they didn't want to entertain the idea that I could be *more* than I was. Sure, in a sense I would never be as healthy and fit as I had been before the accident, but that didn't mean I couldn't be something different *and* better.

I was reminded of the crisis that was created for me when I lost my job with Xerox. I was super stressed by the experience but my obligation to my family forced me to find a solution — and fast. So in an effort to ratchet up the pressure and kickstart the creativity goodies unleashed by crisis I created another crisis by quitting my job!

I was so grateful for that role and they had been so supportive after my accident, but I didn't want to do it anymore so I quit, even though Kate was pregnant again so it wasn't as if she could get a job as a fallback position. I'd been out of the wheelchair for only a few months when I manufactured this new crisis, removed any chance of a safety net, and jumped into the unknown. And this forced me to find opportunities to reinvent my life.

Although I considered myself lucky to be alive, injured or not injured, I did not believe I was the best I could hope for. I know if I had gone along with my rehabilitation team and believed that the best I could hope for was to bounce back to my old life, then my life would not be the way it is today. I had a choice to make: hang on to a job I was no longer passionate about out of fear and gratitude, or create a new crisis and find something better. Remember, necessity is the mother of invention!

## Start bouncing

### *Amplify the frustration*

When you find yourself frustrated or you feel like a problem is looming or you are just annoyed that something didn't happen, use the following thought process to amplify the irritations and turn them into mental crisis. That way you are energised to deal with the situation and you can bounce forward from it.

1. Highlight and focus on the frustration/problem/annoyance.

2. Feel how much it upsets you, how angry you get.

3. Imagine how you would feel if it was resolved.

4. Stop procrastinating and TAKE ACTION — short-term pain for long-term gain.

## Start bouncing

### *The escalation exercise*

Take a moment to think about your current situation. Right now what is the absolute worst thing you can imagine happening? Perhaps it is that you lose another major account or that you lose all your money. Imagine that situation has actually happened. What would you have to do to recover from that situation?

I'm not suggesting you orchestrate such a predicament, but getting into the creative mindset that it would create can be very useful. You don't always have to create the new crisis — just imagining what you might do under those circumstances can be enough to initiate new ideas. Remember the piano experiment — doing the mental work was enough to improve the performance of participants who didn't even touch a piano. So doing the mental work that would be required if you were to experience a crisis can also yield improved results.

## How to ensure that crisis creates opportunity

To bounce forward stronger and better you must learn the five steps of F.O.C.U.S. to ensure that crisis creates opportunity. When crisis comes knocking at your door, F.O.C.U.S. so you can begin a positive turnaround.

» *Futuristic*. Be inspired by strong vision and purpose. Concern yourself only with positive possibilities for the future.

» *Optimistic*. Visualise and expect the best result or outcome all the time. Attitude is everything.

» *Communication*. Effective and efficient communication will always ease the change process. Be honest, be open and be kind to others.

» *Unity*. There must be uniformity and commitment. Everyone *must* be on board and committed to finding a positive outcome.

» *Strategic*. Be strategic in your approach and seek to maximise every opportunity, no matter how obscure or unlikely.

Each step in the F.O.C.U.S. process works together with every other, and not until you have understood, practised and applied each step will you see a positive turnaround. Remember, attitude is everything; everything is attitude.

On 11 September 2001 the world stood still — it was a crisis almost beyond imagining. When the first plane crashed into the World Trade Center in New York, the world was shocked. How could such an accident happen? Then as the second plane crashed into the towers and the world realised it was not an accident the scale of the horror was realised. As far as crises go, September 11 was monumental and the images we saw on that terrible day are seared into our memories forever.

And yet even that crisis created new opportunities. September 11 resulted in a sharp decline in executive travel as people simply did not want to fly to business meetings. When they recognised this shift in behaviour, business partners Tim Duffy and Steve Gandy applied the principles of F.O.C.U.S. Taking a futuristic, optimistic approach, they created MeetingZone to strategically fill the gap in the market by creating a new communication channel for busy executives unwilling to fly.

MeetingZone used the best technology to allow people to collaborate without being in the same physical location — very handy for busy executives who were keen to cut back on their business travel. Rather than video conferencing, which could be patchy and unreliable, they focused on simple, reliable voice conferencing and web collaboration tools. Today MeetingZone is operating in the UK, Germany, Sweden, Canada and the US, with sales in excess of £8.2 million. MeetingZone has gone from strength to strength and for three years running has featured in the *Sunday Times* Microsoft Tech Track 100 list of the fastest growing technology companies in the private sector, with average annual growth rates of 50 to 60 percent.

# The big picture: Adversarial growth

With all the military conflicts and violence in the world, most of us have heard of the term post-traumatic stress disorder (PTSD), a condition particularly related to war experience. Often people who have witnessed horrendous violence and bloodshed are told they will never be the same again.

There is, however, a flip side that psychologists have called post- traumatic growth or adversarial growth. A new body of research indicates that when people are faced with severe adversity such as bereavement, medical transplant, cancer, chronic illness, heart attack, military combat, physical assault or natural disaster, they are often driven to use the crisis to transform their lives in profoundly positive ways.

It's clearly an idea that has been around for a long time — just think of the maxim 'What doesn't kill you makes you stronger' — but it's only been in the past few decades that science and research have begun to build up a solid empirical framework to support it.

Thanks to this research we can now say without question that adversity and severe crisis can lead to great personal growth and positive change across a wide range of experiences. In his brilliant book *The Happiness Advantage*, Shawn Achor cites many examples of this phenomenon in action and suggests that a person's ability to transform crisis into opportunity depends largely on their mindset and their willingness to accept that something good might come of it. Researchers who studied the psychological effects of the Madrid train bombings of 2004 noted, 'It appears that it is not the type of event per se that influences post-traumatic growth, but rather the subjective experience of the event.'

## ADVERSITY HAS THE EFFECT OF ELICITING TALENTS, WHICH IN PROSPEROUS CIRCUMSTANCES WOULD HAVE LAIN DORMANT.
### – HORACE

Bottom line? Only those who have failed in a big way are likely to succeed in a big way. If you shift your perspective and attitude toward crisis, you can see adversity as an invitation to change and reinvent the situation to bounce forward rather than back. As Viktor Frankl puts it, 'What is to give light must endure burning.'

Bounce shows you that crisis can be good. Adversity and challenges can ignite some of the greatest opportunities in your life. Sometimes we need a failure to see the new opportunities that were right in front of us all along.

# CHAPTER 2
# Principle 2: Proximity is power

Personal development speaker and businessman Jim Rohn says, 'You are the average of the five people you spend the most time with.' This theory, known as the *average of five*, applies to just about everything in life — from your weight, your health and your behaviour to your finances and ultimately your success.

In business your success will reflect that of the average of the five closest business colleagues you spend the most time with. In love, your relationships will reflect the average of the five closest friends you spend your time with — are they, for instance, happily married or divorced? You will weigh the average of the five people you spend the most time with. Organisations such as Weight Watchers already know the profound impact existing relationships have on a person's ability to lose weight and regain their health. In fact, friends and family can often be the least supportive, especially if they too are overweight.

Proximity is power.

When I was 16 years old I moved out of home to go and live with my older brother Ben. I was going to college, I couldn't drive and there was no public transport, so I moved in with Ben because his flat was closer to college than my parents' house. I remember one night I decided to have a party. I'd landed the role of Scarecrow in the college production of *The Wizard of Oz* and thought it would be great to invite everyone, so I told my friends and they told their friends. When Ben arrived home that night he could hardly squeeze into his own apartment! That was the night I met Kate and fell in love.

She had agreed to come to the party only because her friend wanted her to ask me out on her friend's behalf. So when we hit it off she felt guilty for betraying her friend's trust and it took weeks before she would agree to go out with me again. Several months later Kate moved into the two-bedroom flat I shared with Ben, and I was over the moon.

My parents, it has to be said, were not. I grew up in a very strict religious household. Although today faith plays a large role in my life, as a teenager I did what most teenagers do and rejected everything my parents held dear. Of course, proximity is powerful in a good way only when the people you are in proximity to are positive people with hopes and aspirations that drive them in a positive direction. Unfortunately proximity is equally powerful in the other direction. In the last few years of school I ended up getting in with the wrong crowd. I wasn't interested in school or getting good qualifications so I could go to university. I didn't have the academic aptitude for it and besides I was much more interested in looking cool and hanging with the fun crowd. I started smoking because all the other kids I was spending time with were smoking, and it wasn't just cigarettes — I was smoking marijuana too. The stupid thing was I hated smoking. I hated the taste and I hated the smell on my clothes, but I persevered because all my mates were smoking and I wanted to fit in.

Once I went to college I moved away from the negative influences and threw myself into college life. I loved the theatre.

I enjoyed singing and dancing, and then when I met Kate it was as though all my Christmases had come at once! I was so excited. I felt so grown up and I revelled in our having our own place. I stopped attending college as regularly and my grades suffered as a result. I didn't notice. I didn't care. I was happy — at least, I thought I was happy. I started smoking weed again, and when I was caught selling a tiny amount to a friend at school they suspended me on the spot. After meeting with the principal I was told that my actions had disgraced the school and I was no longer welcome to study there.

For the next few years Kate and I continued to live together. We both got work so we could move out of Ben's place and rent a place of our own. One by one we lost contact with old friends, the people we'd known in college and the people I'd grown up with, and I fell in with an even worse crowd than I had been around in school.

It all came to a head when I got a job as a duty manager in a pizzeria. I stopped going straight home after work and preferred to go out drinking with my new buddies. After staying out late one day, and with an early shift the following morning, I got home and Kate was waiting for me. She motioned for me to sit down, couldn't meet my eyes and very quietly she said, 'Sam, this isn't working. I don't know where you are at night. I don't know who you're with or what you're doing. This can't go on. You need to make a choice. Either your friends go — or I do.' I chose badly and Kate left.

I was devastated. We'd been together for about three years by then. And then things went from bad to worse. I skipped work and drank too much. Kate had been warning me about my new friends for months but I just thought she was overreacting and jealous. I still remember the night I realised the truth and just how potent proximity really is. One night after my shift I met them for a drink as usual. I had started to notice that it was always me who bought the drinks and it was always me who drove them home because none of them worked or had a car, but it was when they asked me to steal from my employer that I finally woke up.

Their logic was that I had the keys because I was the duty manager. They figured it would be easy for me to slip in, empty the safe and give them the money. Then we would all split it — a team effort. Although I had moved a long way away from my religious upbringing, I knew what they were talking about was wrong and I refused to do it. Undeterred, they suggested that to make it more authentic they would beat me up — just enough so it would look like I'd been counting the cash and just been jumped. I couldn't believe it! In this case, proximity was toxic and I knew I needed to get out.

Finally I realised that Kate had been right all along. I missed her and was determined to win her back. It took willpower to stay away from my old friends, to purposely not visit the places where they hung out and to ignore them when they called in at work to see me, but I did it. And I did it because the crisis I faced reconnected me to a far bigger, more important purpose — Kate. I had become the average of the five people I spent all my time with, and that wasn't anything to be proud of. Now I focused all my energy on turning my life around and proving to Kate I was worthy of her again. Happily I succeeded. We got married on 18 December 1999, just three days after my twentieth birthday! And for the record, I've never smoked anything since.

The company we keep determines who we are. That's as true in business as it is in personal relationships. If you are a negative leader in your business, then your negativity will rub off on others. If you are positive and optimistic, then your proximity will be a powerful reminder to your people for them to be positive and optimistic. Do the people you are working with lift you up or pull you down?

Today I'm acutely aware of the people I spend time with. I know from my own experience that negative influences are like cancer. If we don't root them out early they will spread through our life and career with devastating results. I know just how powerful this principle is and that it could have so easily set me on a very different path.

## Who inspired you?

These days I make sure I surround myself with really positive people who inspire me and challenge me to be more than I was yesterday. People like Brad Smith, Grant Davies and Adam Smith.

At just 16 years old Brad wanted to establish mini motocross Superlite MX in Australia — small bikes with relatively limited grunt that could be ridden by adults and children, or as Brad calls it, 'BMX on steroids!' Initially he imported the bikes from China and sold them to motocross enthusiasts but he didn't think the bikes were good enough, and eventually he travelled around Australia to buy all the bikes back. He then went to China himself to find a manufacturer who could build his dream bike for him. Without funding he was dismissed by countless manufacturers, but he refused to give up and eventually found one company that believed in him and his dream — and the braaap brand — was born. Since then Brad has won several awards including 2010 Tasmanian Young Australian of the Year (in the year after me!), Australian Young Entrepreneur of the Year and runner-up International Young Entrepreneur of the Year. braaap (named after the sound a motocross bike makes) has also won Australian Specialised Retail Business of the Year three times.

In 2008 Brad launched the first braaap retail outlet, intended to be 'the motocross equivalent of a surf shop'. He has since expanded to four retail outlets in Tasmania and Victoria. A franchise model is set to take the brand international. In 2010 braaap signed a deal with NASCAR driver Marcos Ambrose to launch the brand in the US.

Brad is still in his mid twenties. Growing up in housing commission homes he and his sister had great parents who encouraged their children to dream big and follow those dreams no matter what. And he still has time for the passion that started it all; he placed as the highest ranking Australian at the World Mini SX Championships in Las Vegas in 2010, finishing eleventh despite competing against full-time professional riders from around the world. Brad is an awesome guy and my best friend. We talk on the phone two or three times a week.

Then there is Grant Davies, another amazing, inspiring person I speak with regularly. Grant's background is as a dancer, singer and actor. He's been in the entertainment industry for over 20 years. He runs arguably the most successful dance studio in Australia, RGDance, and has had his own comedy show on the Vegas strip at Planet Hollywood at the V Theater. He is also a high performer and we regularly chat and encourage one another.

Adam Smith is another really inspirational guy I just love talking to and spending time with. We really connect through our shared belief in the importance of supporting young people in Australia. Adam is one of Australia's youngest CEOs, leading the Foundation for Young Australians, an independent national grant-making organisation funding and working in partnership with youth- led initiatives. An outstanding advocate for youth development, education and strategic philanthropy, Adam has been recognised through three nominations for Young Australian of the Year; he was also the recipient of a 2004 Celebrating Melbourne Award and was recognised by *The Age* as one of Australia's 40 most influential people under 40.

It wasn't an easy lesson for me to learn and I definitely learned the hard way, but I've come to understand that who you spend time with directly influences who you become, and if you want to manage crisis well and ensure you bounce forward into a better life and greater success, then you need to surround yourself with people who challenge you and ask the hard questions while supporting and encouraging you to find better and better solutions.

**THE PERSON WHO LIVES WITH CRIPPLES WILL SOON LEARN TO LIMP.**

**– ITALIAN PROVERB**

# Habits: Proximity is power

When you find yourself in a crisis, the people you consult and spend your time with will have a profound effect on your ability to navigate the choppy waters successfully. There are therefore certain things you need to do and actions you need to consistently take if you want to emerge stronger than you were prior to the crisis. In short, you need to foster the following habits:

1. Stay connected.

2. Communicate and collaborate.

3. Practise vulnerability.

4. Invest in others.

## 1 STAY CONNECTED

In Shawn Achor's brilliant book *The Happiness Advantage* he tells the story of how in his senior year of high school he completed 90 hours of volunteer firefighter training. The final test was called the Fire Maze, where the rookies would come face to face with a real-life, full-scale fire. Inside an old farm silo called the Smoke Tank was a massive wooden maze with 10-foot-high walls and plenty of flammable material lying around to add authenticity and unpredictability to the blaze. The maze was set on fire and Achor and his partner were ordered inside in their flame-repellent suits and oxygen masks. The instructions were simple: there was a dummy 'trapped' in the middle of the maze and their goal was to rescue the dummy and get out of the blaze safely. They were reminded that in almost zero visibility it is extremely easy to get disoriented, and the only way to avoid getting lost was to keep in constant contact with the wall. The pair was to enter the silo holding on to each other so one could maintain contact with the wall while the other searched the ground for the dummy.

Achor and his partner were assured that as a pair they could complete the task in about seven to 10 minutes, but there was one hour's worth of oxygen in their tanks just in case. As an extra precaution an alarm would sound when they were down to their final five minutes of oxygen, so if they did get lost they would need to get out immediately once they heard the alarm.

Initially things went well. They followed the instructions and made slow progress, although they hadn't yet found the dummy. Then the alarm went off on his partner's oxygen tank, followed closely by his own. Neither had realised they had been in the silo for so long and their confusion added to their disorientation, so they started to panic. Despite all the instructions Achor let go of his partner and his partner let go of the wall! Alone and terrified, they called out to each other but neither could hear the other. Within a few minutes both were rescued by veteran firefighters and hauled outside to safety.

The 90-day training always ended with the newbies having to be rescued. There wasn't a dummy to find and the alarms were deliberately set to go off early to initiate panic and confusion. Once panic and confusion set in the two new firefighters always let go of each other and the rescuers always found them circling in a dead end about 20 feet from each other, waiting to die!

When the going gets tough, why is it that we let go of the people who can help us the most?

If you want to survive the heat of a crisis and bounce forward into a better life, then you must stay connected. And perhaps staying connected will become a little easier in future simply knowing that your initial reaction will be to let go.

It's unclear why crisis can often initiate a disconnection from others at the very time that they are needed most. Perhaps our survival instinct kicks in and we feel we stand a better chance if we have only ourselves to worry about. Perhaps we feel embarrassed — this is probably especially true for us men, who don't like to admit we've made a mistake. Certainly if you look at the example of 'rogue traders' who have lost millions, sometimes billions for their employers, they are all men.

Take Nick Leeson, for example. He bought and sold futures (complex financial derivatives) on the SIMEX exchange in Singapore and made huge profits for Barings Bank. Then he made a few mistakes and rather than tell anyone, he disconnected and tried to fix the errors himself. In a final effort to rectify the losses he'd accumulated, on 16 January 1995 he bet big on the Japanese market going up. Unfortunately for him and the oldest investment bank in the UK, on 17 January Japan was rocked by a massive earthquake and the Japanese market tanked. Barings collapsed under the weight of $827 million losses and Leeson went to prison.

Leeson's losses, however, look like pocket change compared with more recent financial crises such as those of Bear Stearns, Lehman Brothers, Société Générale and UBS. And while the amount of money lost by so-called rogue traders increases, the general sequence remains the same: an initial error or misdemeanour is covered up and the trader in the middle of the crisis disconnects from those around him, which allows a relatively small, recoverable error to escalate into a full-scale financial disaster. In the financial world of huge bonuses and even bigger egos it's easy to see why these individuals didn't want to speak up, but disconnecting was the wrong choice.

Of course, disconnection in times of crisis is by no means a male- only trait. Men and women are equally susceptible. We only have a limited amount of energy, so when crisis arrives it can often feel as though we need to pull back all that available energy to make sure we get through the crisis. Anything not considered absolutely necessary is therefore sidelined, and the casualties are often friendships, work relationships and family connections. So we stop chatting to our friends, we stop meeting colleagues for lunch or catching up after work, and instead we eat lunch at our desk and work till 2 am in an effort to find a solution. But what we can so easily forget is that these connections don't just require our energy; they nurture us and give us more energy, and they help us to think differently, and perhaps to relax a little so we can get greater access to the solutions we seek. Studies show, for example, that each positive interaction employees have during the working day helps return the cardiovascular system to normal resting levels, thus reducing the amount of cortisol or stress hormone in their system. Also, those with strong relationships are less susceptible to stress in the first place.

When times are hard and you find yourself in the middle of a crisis, hold on tight to your professional and social networks because they will help you to get through the ordeal quicker and with less stress. Besides, sometimes laughter really is the best medicine.

I've always been a bit of a joker and that hasn't changed since my accident. I remember when my oldest brother, Stephen, my mentor and good friend for most of my life, arrived at the hospital for the first time. While I'd been unconscious, the doctors had told Kate and my family that they suspected I'd suffered brain damage in the crash and I might have lost some of my mental capacity. Luckily I hadn't suffered any head injuries other than some cuts and bruises so I was okay, but Stephen didn't know that. I was awake when he came into my room and I could tell he was shocked by what he saw but was trying desperately to look as though everything was fine. I didn't react. He came closer and almost whispered, 'Sam, what have you done!' I still didn't react.

By this point he was almost by my bedside, still speaking, trying to elicit a response from me. I looked at him blankly, saying nothing, then asked, 'Who are you? Do I know you?' His face fell and I burst out laughing, even though it hurt when I laughed. His face lit up and he started laughing too, relieved that I was obviously just the same old Sammy he knew.

My reaction to my injuries gave my family and friends permission to be okay too. If I'd pushed them away I would have made a difficult time for them even harder and I'm sure I would have made what was a difficult time for me exponentially more so.

**THE WORLD IS SO EMPTY IF ONE THINKS ONLY OF MOUNTAINS, RIVERS AND CITIES; BUT TO KNOW SOMEONE WHO THINKS AND FEELS WITH US, AND WHO, THOUGH DISTANT, IS CLOSE TO US IN SPIRIT, THIS MAKES THE EARTH FOR US AN INHABITED GARDEN.**

**– GOETHE**

## Start bouncing

### Hold hands in the fire

Take a moment to think of a problem or difficulty you are currently experiencing. It could be a personal problem or a business challenge. Identify who you are most likely to disconnect from during this difficult time. Consider diarising contacts with these people so you don't end up isolating yourself from the people you need the most during your transition.

## 2 COMMUNICATE AND COLLABORATE

After my accident I was in hospital for five months, which meant that for a time there I became like part of the furniture. I was gradually improving although it wasn't a linear process. I'd have good days and bad days, but mainly they were good days. My doctors were still warning me that I was going to 'hit the wall' emotionally, but as far as I was concerned hitting the car was enough and I wasn't keen to hit anything else for quite some time.

I had so many visitors the nurses were getting a little annoyed, but being with people and sharing my situation made it so much easier for everyone. I remember one friend who told me that he had arrived at the hospital with a plan. He was sure I would be depressed so he was going to lift my spirits no matter what. He later told me that he felt that I'd lifted his spirits and inspired him, and he started to visit regularly because he enjoyed my company. It was during this time that I really started to realise the power of proximity, how infectious my optimism was for others and how important bounce really was to the wider community.

Don't get me wrong. My rehabilitation was really tough. I'd gone from being an incredibly independent person, travelling all over the country advising government on youth employment trends, to needing help going to the toilet. The painkillers meant that I couldn't feel my body a lot of the time and my mind hadn't yet adapted to the fact that large parts either were no longer there or just didn't work the same. I'd try to pick up drinks with my right arm — I still do it now, although having a bionic arm certainly helps. I also endured countless operations and hours and hours of relentless physiotherapy and occupational therapy. I would work for hours on my exercises, building muscle in my legs, learning how to use various prosthetics on my arm. It was gruelling work and the pain was pretty intense at times. I had dozens of operations on my leg — they put in pins and plates, wired me back together and took me apart again. It was agony, but as much as possible I avoided painkillers. I learned to manage the pain on my own. From my past I knew what could happen to people who used drugs too much for too long, how it could affect their body and brain, and I didn't want that for me. If I was going to recover, then I was going to do it my way. It wasn't all plain sailing, though. I'd make progress and then slip back and it was extremely disheartening at times, but I refused to let it get me down for long.

The more I tried, the more I realised I could still do what I wanted. I could still feed myself, I could still talk on the phone, and with the help of wheelchairs and crutches I could still move around, albeit slowly.

My attitude was so surprising to so many people that I became known as the 'in-house counsellor' for the hospital and would often go and speak to other patients. One in particular stands out for me. Tony (we'll call him) had lost his leg in a terrible motorcycle accident. He wasn't taking it well at all. He'd even tried to commit suicide. His doctors and the nurses had tried to talk to get him to open up but he refused. Specialist counsellors had been called in but nothing was working so I was asked to go and talk to him. By this point I was up and moving around and I'd been given an electric scooter to help me get around. So I took my scooter up to Tony's room and started talking to him. The doctors and professionals may have known theoretically what he was going through and they may have known about the stages of grief, but knowing something from a book and really knowing it deep in your soul are two very different things. All Tony wanted was to talk to someone who really understood what he was feeling. He wanted to be able to talk about his fears without judgement and to work with someone who could help him find his own path through his crisis. Over the coming weeks we laughed together, we cried together and we had wheelchair races in the corridor together. He inspired me and I inspired him and together we came out of our respective crises stronger and better people. He just needed to know someone cared and someone positive and optimistic was there.

My doctors and nurses told me frequently that my determination not only to get better but to surpass my old life was encouraging other patients to fight harder, to be more enthusiastic about their own condition and to design their own future by their own rules. Often all they really needed was someone to communicate and collaborate with!

Whatever crisis you find yourself in, whether professional or personal, you must keep communicating and collaborating with others. Take losing your job, for example. When someone experiences the crisis of redundancy they often feel embarrassed or ashamed, even if there is no reason for it and the redundancy was due only to company-wide cutbacks. These feelings cause the individual to cut off from the people he or she knows. This is exactly the opposite of what needs to happen, if you are to find a new job quickly. We all know that many people find work through the connections and contacts they already have with past colleagues, employers or other business or personal contacts. And yet when we are down or upset we turn away from those vital connections.

Sadly when we face a crisis our natural instinct is often to withdraw, thus disconnecting from the people best able to support us. And we stop talking. Nothing can amplify a crisis more than silence.

In business we are often encouraged to keep our problems to ourselves and to leave our emotions at the door, but business is a collection of people, and people are a collection of emotions, so telling people to leave their emotions at the door is a little like asking them not to breathe while they are at the office.

We are social creatures and we need to communicate and collaborate. If you or your team are experiencing difficulties at work, you are much more likely to find a solution if you communicate those challenges honestly and openly and seek a collective solution. What normally happens, however, is that communication stops completely! Unfortunately, gossip does not and the void created by the lack of real communication and information will be fuelled by negativity and unhelpful speculation. Just think about this for a moment. If your boss stops you unexpectedly and asks to see you in his office, where does your mind go? If your partner calls you at work and leaves a message that you need to call back urgently, where does your mind go?

Left to its own devices — without adequate information and communication — your brain is instinctively pessimistic. Considering that the oldest part of your brain is concerned only with your survival, this initial instinct is normal but you need to manage it. Going quiet in a crisis won't help you and it won't help the people around you, so stay connected, reach out, stay in communication and collaborate to come up with possible solutions.

Maintaining open communication channels will also do wonders for accountability. I think one of the most powerful things you can do in your life is to communicate your dreams and goals to others. The reason we don't communicate is often because we don't want to be held to account. Many fall short of these dreams and aspirations because we can't admit and tell others how much we want something. If you share your challenge and explain your plan and what you are going to do with the people around you, then every time you see those people they will ask you how you are getting on. It can be uncomfortable but that discomfort can be used to great effect.

Crisis has a powerful way of connecting you to your purpose and re-familiarising you with your why. Once you share that why through open and honest communication you will always be held to a higher standard than you would have been had you stayed silent.

When it comes to working through crisis, dealing with difficult situations or achieving goals and delivering on plans, communicating those plans to others is crucial. Keeping those plans to yourself may reduce the fear of failure and public scrutiny, but it also makes it far too easy to avoid taking the necessary action and making the hard choices. Everyone is much more likely to keep their commitments if they have communicated those commitments publicly.

They are also much more likely to follow through on those commitments if they collaborate with colleagues or friends. In a study conducted by Simone Schnall from the University of Plymouth, subjects were taken to the bottom of a hill and asked to estimate how steep it was and how difficult it would be to climb. What was particularly interesting was that when the person was able to collaborate and make the journey with a friend he or she estimated the hill to be 15 percent lower than when they had to estimate on their own. Even thinking about a friend before making the estimate made the hill look less daunting!

Human beings are better in groups. We are more inventive and more creative when we can bounce ideas off each other. Challenges seem less daunting and together we are better able to negotiate difficulty. When we think of someone like Thomas Edison, we imagine a lone figure in a dusty workshop inventing away and yet the truth is very different. Edison was part of a huge team — he communicated and collaborated himself into the history books.

## Start bouncing

### *Deliberate pessimism*

Relating to your current challenge, take a moment to stand in the shoes of each of the people you identified in the earlier exercise 'Start bouncing: Hold hands in the fire'. Based on what you have already shared with them about what is going on, what is the worst they are imagining right now? If you find this hard, then imagine the roles were reversed and the other person had your challenge and they had communicated and collaborated with you as much as you had with them. What would you be thinking right now?

When left in the dark we will always assume the worst. Take steps to rectify the situation and get back in communication with the necessary people.

## 3 PRACTISE VULNERABILITY

We are born vulnerable. Our survival depends on someone taking care of us so essentially we have no choice. A baby doesn't worry and panic about how quickly he or she is going to walk. The parents might. They might start comparing notes with friends and relatives but the child doesn't think about it. As children we are happy to learn, fall down, look silly, get up and start again. Then we grow up and all that changes and the vulnerability is suppressed. By the time we reach early adulthood most of us consider vulnerability to be a weakness, especially in business. If you look as though you don't know what you're doing then you won't get the promotion. If you ask for help you will be considered incompetent and there is a huge amount of pressure to perform to a particular standard. In business there is often no room for vulnerability and that's a huge mistake. It's the reason behind the Peter Principle.

The Peter Principle is the recognition that a business that promotes on achievement and ability will eventually promote individuals to roles *beyond* their ability, at which point they cease to be promoted further. Once someone gets into a role that is beyond them they won't ask for help, which simply accelerates their decline. It's also the reason corporate training rarely sticks and it's the reason that people don't like change.

When a child takes his first tentative steps or hauls himself up onto a chair, planting his face in the chair to do so, his parents are usually standing by squealing with joy and gushing encouragement. If the child falls flat on his face his mother doesn't immediately announce that all walking from now on is cancelled and he needs to just sit on the chair and forget he ever tried. She lavishes him with praise and the little boy tries again.

Compare that with how you feel when you are asked to do something new at work or the reaction you meet when you ask your team to start using a new software program. What you feel or witness is vulnerability, which will manifest as irritation, ridicule, boredom or outright hostility. In order for us to learn and grow we need to be as open and vulnerable as a child, but because we see vulnerability as a sign of weakness we refuse to show it, so we don't grow!

This difference in mindset has been the life's work of world-renowned Stanford University psychologist Carol Dweck. In her book *Mindset: The New Psychology of Success*, Dweck writes that she was 'obsessed with understanding how people cope with failures'. Her early research involved investigating how children reacted to puzzles they were asked to solve. She was immediately struck by how different children and adults view 'failure'. Dweck had expected to find that, like adults, some children would cope well when they couldn't solve the puzzles and others would not cope well. But what she found was that if the children were young enough, none of them considered not being able to solve the puzzle a failure in the first place. Instead it was considered a fun challenge. Dweck proposes that everything in your life comes down to your mindset and there are only two — fixed and growth.

If you have a fixed mindset, then you believe that you were born with certain aptitudes and abilities and that they are fixed by your genes or upbringing. If you have smart parents, you'll be smart. If you don't then you won't. People with a fixed mindset believe either you've got it or you haven't, and if you missed out on the genetic lottery then there is nothing you can do to change that. It's easy to see why vulnerability in this context is seen as such a bad thing. As Dweck says, 'If you have only a certain amount of intelligence, a certain personality, and a certain moral character — well, then you'd better prove that you have a healthy dose of them. It simply wouldn't do to look or feel deficient in these most basic characteristics.' Vulnerability is therefore a big no-no.

If you have a growth mindset, on the other hand, you don't believe your aptitudes and abilities are genetically or socially predetermined. If you have a growth mindset you see those abilities as the starting point from which to expand and develop through effort, perseverance and practice. They represent the start line, not the finish line, and the real finish will depend on individual effort.

We are all born with a growth mindset. Children know that learning is essential and they don't freak out when they are in a new situation. They don't care if they fall or look silly or people laugh — they laugh too and try again. Children are not threatened and they don't mind being vulnerable. Then the judgements, opinions, expectations and prejudices begin to filter into their consciousness and somewhere around 12 years old they begin to change.

Unfortunately we are trained in the fixed mindset from a very early age. Just think about it. Were you praised for being smart or were you praised for your effort? Most of us got smiley faces and gold stars for perfect scores, not for trying our hardest. On the sports field we are rewarded for winning, not for taking part. We tell our children it's taking part that matters and having fun that counts, but it's the winners who get the medals. In short, we are taught that failure is unacceptable and our vulnerability is suppressed for good.

When you are in a crisis, you are by definition in a new situation. You don't know what to do and you probably need to find new information and come up with new ideas and solutions. That can be almost impossible if we refuse to admit our vulnerability, to accept we have fallen short and to reach out for help and alternatives.

I remember a few years ago I was in a real pickle financially. I'd never been good with money and Kate and I had always muddled through, but it was a hand-to-mouth existence and as our family grew this caused more and more stress. Neither of us had really been taught how to manage money. My parents have refused to own property or use credit cards because they feel it somehow interferes with their connection with God. In religious circles money is often perceived as negative, even though the Bible says it is *the love of* money that is the root of all evil, which is very different from money itself being the root of all evil. When I was growing up we had very little money and we used to grow a lot of our own food. And Kate's parents didn't teach her about money either so we were both clueless.

I hated talking about it and it would often be a source of tension in our home. I didn't want to admit that I wasn't able to provide for my family; besides we always seemed to manage. The idea of being vulnerable around my weaknesses in money management was standing in the way of my finding a permanent solution. Over time it just got worse and worse until I finally cracked. I looked around at my networks to see who I knew who was good with money and had been financially successful. It wasn't easy and I had to swallow my pride, but I also realised that I needed to admit my vulnerability to the people in proximity to me in order to grow and develop not just myself but those relationships. Plus I was determined to provide for my family so I guess my why was big enough to spur me into action. I needed to learn new strategies around money and before I could really grow and develop I first needed to admit I didn't have any strategies around money. So I contacted a friend and asked him for help. Within a year Kate and I had bought our first house — an exciting beginning to a life that is now no longer dictated by money.

There's a great joke about a religious man who finds himself in the middle of a storm. As the water level rises he climbs up onto his roof. Sitting in the rain with a blanket around him he sees a man in a canoe paddling past and the man shouts out, 'Hey, get in the boat and I'll take you to safety.' The man on the roof replies, 'Thank you but I'm fine. God is going to save me.' The man in the canoe shrugs his shoulders and paddles on to help someone else. A few hours go by and the water is still rising and a helicopter appears above him and drops a ladder down. The man in the helicopter shouts down to the man on the roof, 'Hey, climb on the ladder and I'll take you to safety.' The man on the roof replies, 'Thank you but I'm fine. God is going to save me.' The man in the helicopter shrugs his shoulders and flies on to help someone else. A few hours pass and the water is lapping at his feet and a powerboat roars up to the man and the captain shouts, 'Hey, get in the boat I'll take you to safety.' Again the man on the roof replies, 'Thank you but I'm fine. God is going to save me.' The man in the powerboat shrugs his shoulders and powers on to help someone else. Within minutes the man drowns. Soon he finds himself at the Pearly Gates speaking to God. 'Where were you?' yells the man. 'I have believed in you all my life and I believed you'd save me but you didn't. Where were you?' God looks at the man and says, 'Who do you think sent the canoe, the helicopter and the powerboat?'

They say that God helps those who help themselves. Whether you believe in God or not, you must reach out and ask for help. You must learn to foster a growth mindset and become friends with vulnerability. It takes courage and real strength to admit when we are wrong and we need help. Also, people warm to this type of authenticity and that also helps to open doors and break down barriers. No-one likes a smart-arse know-it-all anyway, so why do we feel compelled to appear invincible?

## Start bouncing

### The canoe, helicopter and powerboat test

Someone, somewhere in your networks right now already knows how to solve your problems. There are canoes, helicopters and powerboats at the ready just waiting for you to drop your defences and get creative and determined about solving your crisis. Consider the challenge you currently face. Who do you know, right now, who may be able to help or point you in the right direction? Write down five names.

## 4 INVEST IN OTHERS

If you are influenced by the people in your proximity, then it follows that the people in your sphere are also influenced by you. The Proximity is Power principle is a two-way street and in order for it to really gain momentum you need to foster positive habits that influence in both directions. The previous three habits relate to what you can do and how you can open yourself up to solutions and support so you can positively benefit from what others can bring to the crisis. This habit is about making sure that you nurture and support other people so they also benefit from the interaction.

One of the most significant insights I've ever come across in this regard was offered by Gary Chapman's wonderful book *The 5 Love Languages*. Although he talks about love specifically, they are just as relevant to any relationship — with colleagues or peers as well as in personal friendships and relationships.

Chapman proposes that each of us communicate via five key languages of love, which are:

» words of affirmation

» acts of service

» receiving gifts

» quality time

» physical touch.

Usually we will have one or two primary love languages that act as our preferred modes of communication. So each person has a default operating system when it comes to receiving and demonstrating love and care for another person.

If your primary language of love is words of affirmation, then you thrive on compliments and conversation. You will want someone to notice what you have done or changes you've made and verbally acknowledge them.

If your primary language of love is acts of service, then you feel loved when other people do things for you. My primary language of love is acts of service. I love it when I come home and the house is tidy and my evening meal is ready. I love that my clothes are washed and ironed and ready for me when I need them. It makes me feel cared for and appreciated. In the office I really appreciate it if someone helps me out with emails or tidies my office, because these little acts of service push my buttons and make me feel good.

My mum's primary language of love was also acts of service, which is probably why it's now such a big deal for me. When I was a child my mum never told me that she loved me and I don't remember being hugged. But I never doubted that I was loved, because her way of demonstrating her love for us was that she would cook a beautiful meal every night and we could eat as much as we wanted. On the flip side acts of service were also the way she wanted us to demonstrate our love for her. So we had chores and she was always really happy when we did our chores well. When we did we effectively talked to her in her own language. It wouldn't have mattered much if we had tried to give her a hug or tell her we loved her, because it was only when we demonstrated acts of service to her that she felt fully appreciated or loved. For people like my mum and myself, actions really do speak louder than words.

For other people receiving gifts is a critical way they feel loved and it's the way they demonstrate love to others. The size or scale of the gift is usually not that relevant, but the act of working out what might be the best gift, scouring the shops for the perfect present, finding the wrapping paper and writing the card are all part of the ritual. Often the giving of a gift is more enjoyable than the receiving for these people. Often they will have tears in their eyes as they hand over this exquisitely wrapped gift, which is exactly what you wanted or needed but you didn't even know!

Kate's primary language is quality time. She loves just snuggling up with me and the kids on the couch as we watch some TV. It doesn't matter what's on TV or whether or not we are talking; she thrives on undivided attention. Nothing irritates her more than if I'm supposed to be chilling out with her and the kids and I take phone calls or fire up the laptop and work on emails. When I'm physically with Kate she wants me to be mentally and emotionally with her too. That's her definition of quality time.

Finally, physical touch is the language of love of people who need contact in order to feel loved. These people are usually physically demonstrative. In a personal setting they will respond to hugs and hold hands, and in a professional setting they will make a point of shaking your hand or hugging you (if the situation is appropriate). They might also touch your forearm in meetings or put a hand on your shoulder. In a world of politically incorrect contact it's these people who have the hardest time in a workplace, because often any type of physical touch can be misinterpreted.

When I first learned about the languages of love it made so much sense. And the insights are especially powerful when you relate them to others. As a leader navigating a crisis you need to relate to others, inspire them and influence them to engage and navigate the crisis with you. And that often means working out how to get the best out of people and to make sure that they feel supported and nurtured.

It may initially seem a little odd to talk about the languages of love in a work setting, but think of them as the languages of cooperation. If you want your people to feel cared for and appreciated so *they* also stay connected, communicate and collaborate and allow themselves to be a little vulnerable, then you need to relate to them in a way that resonates with them rather than necessarily in a way that resonates with you.

My primary language is acts of service, so I feel most appreciated and connected when other people go out their way to help me out with tasks and things I need. I used to repay that kindness by doing my own acts of service for that person. We've all heard the biblical injunction 'Do unto others as you would have them do unto you'. Only when it comes to love and appreciation it's different!

If I am ever tempted to demonstrate my love and appreciation for Kate by making an evening meal at the weekend or fixing the dripping tap in the bathroom, she might be pleasantly surprised but it won't mean that much to her. I might be sitting around feeling very pleased with myself, thinking how great I've been, but I didn't speak to her in her language. I spoke to her in my language and so the message got lost in translation. However, because I know her language is quality time if I really want to make her feel loved and I know she's tired, for example, then I might arrange for a friend or family member to come over and mind the kids for the evening while we go to a hotel and have dinner, with no mobile phone, and then stay the night and just hang out together. That would be more meaningful to her than my doing my own ironing for the next ten years.

The reason we are so often disappointed by others is that they don't talk to us in our language. And it's such a shame because the intention of care is often present; it's just being expressed in a form that the other person doesn't recognise or understand.

In business you have to go out of your way to find out what languages your people speak, and you need to deliver your messages of appreciation and encouragement in a language that works for the person you are communicating with, not just in a language you relate to. Physical touch in the workplace can be fraught with misunderstanding, but most people have two primary languages of love, so focus on the language most appropriate to each of your team members and demonstrate your commitment and care in that language. In this way they will feel valued and appreciated, which will further accelerate your collective ability to face any crisis and find appropriate solutions that help everyone. Proximity is power is not just about how other people influence you; it is about actively seeking ways for you to help and support others in your sphere of influence. Find ways to give back — even if it's just taking the time to work out their language so you can ensure that they feel valued and part of the team.

## Start bouncing

### What's their language?

Take a moment to think about each of your team members. Taking each in turn, if you have to guess, what do you think their primary language is? There are often clues in their behaviour. So someone whose language is physical touch will always shake hands or hug others. Those who respond to words of affirmation will light up if you compliment them. If someone has written them a note or sent a card they may keep it on display in their workstation for months. Those who respond to quality time will actively seek out meetings with you and want your undivided attention — even for a few minutes a day.

*(Continued)*

> **Start bouncing** (*Cont'd*)
>
> Those who respond to gifts may bring in cakes or bags of sweets for the office. Those who respond to acts of service will often go out of their way to meet visitors to the office and ask them if they would like a coffee or a glass of water.

## How to ensure that proximity is power

To bounce forward stronger than ever, you need to embody the five

P.O.W.E.R. traits to ensure that proximity translates into positive power to create an amazing life:

» *Positive.* Achievers are attracted to and rejuvenated by exceptionally positive people.

» *Outstanding.* Seek to stand out; don't conform or accept mediocrity. Always push for better. Always push for greatness.

» *Willing.* Take risks, try new things and accept that failure is always part of success. Help others wherever you can and expect doors to open.

» *Enthusiastic.* Be passionate and excited about living an outrageously awesome life.

» *Reliable.* Be someone others trust and can count on. Never judge. Be ready to lend a hand. Be generous.

Each step in the P.O.W.E.R. process works together with the others, and not until you have understood, practised and applied each trait will you reap the benefits of proximity in your own life. Be the type of person others are attracted to and other great people will open doors for you in ways you wouldn't have believed possible. Remember, attitude is everything; everything is attitude.

Everyone has heard the expression, 'It's not what you know, but who you know.' The implication is that experience, knowledge and education will always come second to relationships. It is people, relationships, networks and connections that really make the world go round.

It was American social psychologist Stanley Milgram who popularised the hypothesis of a shrinking world and demonstrated just how true that idea really is. Milgram suggested that each person is connected to everyone else within six steps or connections. In his 1967 'small world experiment' he sent packages to random people in Omaha, Nebraska. Each person was asked to forward the package to a person they knew on a first-name basis who they thought might get the package closer to its final destination — a stockbroker in Boston, Massachusetts. This idea of reaching out and accessing friends and acquaintances who can then reach out and access other people is the basis of many of the social networks that now exist.

In the 1960s Milgram used snail mail; today, with new technology and almost infinite access to vast networks, it's likely that far fewer than six degrees would be needed. I have a theory that today we are all connected by only *three* degrees of separation — that every human on the planet can access every other person through three connections. I have not tested this theory but social networks have certainly reduced our degrees of separation. One study done by Ipsos Global Public Affairs in January 2013 showed that more than 85 percent of the world is connected to a social network or an email, which means it's highly likely we can get in contact with almost any person in the world in just a few clicks. Pretty cool, eh!

Reid Hoffman applied a similar theory to create LinkedIn, one of the most successful social networking sites, during an economic downturn. His achievement was especially impressive given that he was creating a technology-based business in the aftermath of the dot.com technology crash of the early 2000s. LinkedIn was created to give people access to the 'who you know' part of the equation by linking people professionally so they could source work, find opportunities and expand business. According to a LinkedIn press release in January 2013 they have more than 200 million members in over 200 countries and territories, and the company claims that two people join LinkedIn every second!

As a testament to the philosophy that proximity is power, LinkedIn and other social networking sites have reduced the six degrees of separation by two or three degrees! The site allows you to leave endorsements and testimonials. You can immediately see who you are connected to and who the people you are connected to are connected to. In fact, of the 25000 'requests for introduction' in mid 2005, 87 percent were accepted. In *MIT Tech Review* Michael Fitzgerald relates the story of how a media and technology marketing consultant in San Francisco read about a company he thought should be his client. He entered the company name into LinkedIn and found he was already connected to four people in the company. The consultant then wrote his proposal and sent it to the person who had contact with the CEO. Four hours later he got an email from the CEO requesting a meeting!

Proximity is power.

## The big picture: People power

It was Harry F. Harlow, professor of psychology at the University of Wisconsin, who first raised questions about human motivation in the 1940s. He and his colleagues discovered that monkeys would solve puzzles without reward or threat of punishment. Clearly, solving puzzles did not impact on the monkeys' survival so something else was happening. Harlow suggested that there must be another motivating drive for which the completion of those tasks was reward in itself.

Harlow's insights had a direct influence on the work of MIT management professor Douglas McGregor and also Abraham Maslow, a student of Harlow's, who famously went on to develop Maslow's hierarchy of needs. In the 1970s psychologist and motivation specialist Edward Deci, along with Richard developed self-determination theory (SDT), which sought to explain the third motivational drive hinted at by Harlow in the 1940s. Deci and Ryan believed that motivation comes from our human need for:

» autonomy

» competence

» relatedness.

When these needs are met we are motivated, happy, creative and productive. Motivated, happy, creative and productive people are better able to solve crises. If these needs are not met, then things have a tendency to go pear-shaped. Their absence causes or at least intensifies crisis.

I'll explain the relevance of autonomy and competence in chapter 4, but in relation to the idea that proximity is power, the power comes from our need for relatedness.

Sport illustrates well how inspiring it can be to be part of a group with a shared vision. When we are connected to other people we respect, admire and care about, we are capable of far more than we would ever be on our own. We are each of us a collection of relationships that we create in our lives — with family, friends and colleagues, people we meet for a season and people we know for a lifetime — and we need these connections to feel happy and productive.

There is nothing unexpected about relatedness, other than the fact that the very thing we need most — other people — is often the first thing we push away in a crisis. We all know intellectually that 'no man is an island' and we appreciate that achieving anything requires the help and cooperation of others, but we will often hit the 'eject' button the moment a crisis arrives. And that is absolutely the worst thing we can do.

It's clear from a vast array of research in the social sciences that we do better in groups. We need to connect with people and those connections are especially important during a crisis. Our instinct may be to batten down the hatches and disconnect from others, but if we do then we will almost certainly make it harder to cope with the crisis and will probably extend it more than is necessary.

Looking back to my accident I am often amazed and awed by Kate's calm response; I know the doctors thought it was miraculous.

One day my curiosity got the better of me and I asked her how she was able to deal with all the uncertainty around my condition so serenely. She said, 'I was never uncertain about whether you would wake up or not. I was more uncertain about how you would react when you woke up. But the doctors said to me that the most important thing was how you saw me react.'

What a powerful insight. In a crisis we look to each other for guidance, reassurance and support and if we don't receive that, then the crisis can be amplified a hundredfold. It was important for my recovery that Kate remained calm and optimistic, and there's no doubt her strength and courage spurred me toward a faster recovery.

The same happens in business all the time. Too often as leaders we worry about how the team will react to the crisis, but they are taking their lead in how to react by watching you.

Proximity is power has a cumulative effect — either positively or negatively. It is your job, therefore, to ensure that you foster the habits that will lead you and your team into a positive spiral upward instead of a negative spiral downward.

If you hide yourself away in your office and refuse to communicate or collaborate, your team will fill in the gaps in their knowledge with gossip and negativity. If you refuse to acknowledge any effort that others make to solve the problem, they will stop trying. If, on the other hand, you stay connected to your team, communicate the challenge and seek collaboration to find the answers, allow yourself to be vulnerable and celebrate the wins along the way, then you will be astonished at what emerges.

# CHAPTER 3
# Principle 3: Leveraging positivity to fuel success

As discussed in the introduction of this book, a crisis situation can take many forms. It can slowly creep up on us over time or it can happen in a heartbeat. Either way, once it arrives we are painfully aware of it. With the right mindset we can turn any crisis into an opportunity, especially if we embrace the principle Proximity is Power. But transitioning out of crisis rarely means flicking a switch or making a single decision that will miraculously lift us out of the crisis unscathed. We need to accept that change will not normally happen overnight but instead will be the result of strong, consistent action toward a new horizon. Transition from crisis to opportunity is a journey, and that journey is not always straightforward.

After five months in hospital I was allowed to go home. The occupational therapy team working with my insurance company had been to my home and several modifications had been made to the house to help me adjust. They had installed ramps and knocked out internal walls so I could get around more easily, and they had arranged for a new bathroom to be fitted. My office was also remodelled. The team really did an amazing job.

I was over the moon when I was told I could go home. The thought of sleeping in my own bed and waking up in the morning with my family around me — it felt like I'd won the lottery. When I arrived home via a special taxi that could accommodate wheelchairs it was obvious Kate and the girls had been busy. They'd put up big banners saying 'Welcome Home Dad', there was a streamer along the wall and balloons hung from the rafters. As my driver helped me out of the taxi Kate and the girls ran toward me and for a moment we were all a tangle of arms and legs. I was home — at last!

The road to recovery was long and it took me several more months at home before I was able to take my first unassisted steps. I was thrilled when I managed it, though. Once I was upright again there was no stopping me, and if walking became too slow I'd hop on my good leg instead. By June, the start of Australian winter, there was a magical coating of frost outside. I had been asked out for breakfast by a friend so I'd got up early and was getting ready to go and meet him at a local café. I wrapped up against the elements, kissed Kate goodbye and headed out of the house at about 6.30 am. As usual I was in a bit of a rush; still operating on pre-accident thinking I'd underestimated how long it would take to get ready. As I left the house and made my way to the car the unthinkable happened. My leg slipped on the ice and came out from under me. As I fell my already injured leg flipped out to one side and I heard something 'crack'. My heart sank.

The pain was incredible and as I lay there, unable to move, I was utterly overwhelmed. I just couldn't believe it! I'd come so far and worked so hard and it seemed so cruel to suffer another injury now, just as I was gathering forward momentum.

I screamed for Kate to come and help me. In a heartbeat she was by my side and we could see panic in each other's eyes.

I couldn't get up and I knew I would have to go back to hospital. I was devastated. In a way this felt even worse than my original accident. I was upset and angry with myself for not being more careful and tears began to run down my cheeks. I'd worked and trained and sweated and screamed to be able to come home and now I would have to go back. It wasn't fair. If I'd broken my leg again, and from the initial sound and the pain I was pretty sure I had, then there would be more surgery, more assessments, more doctors and tests and physiotherapy. I didn't know how long I would be in there for this time.

Eventually the ambulance arrived and I was whisked away to hospital where I went through the usual round of tests and X-rays. My regular doctor wasn't there that morning but another doctor examined the results and told me, 'You've been lucky. It looks like it's just a really bad sprain. You haven't broken it again.' I have to confess I didn't feel that lucky in that moment, and although I was relieved I wasn't convinced he was right. I was sure I'd heard something snap and later when I was discharged even getting home was agony. They had given me crutches but have you ever tried using crutches with one arm?

As the days passed the pain worsened. Within two days my leg had swollen up. I had questioned the doctor at the time and he was adamant I hadn't broken it, but if I hadn't then why was the pain getting worse rather than better? Within about a week of the fall I got a phone call from the hospital. My usual doctor was back and he'd gone over my X-rays and test results again and he wanted to come and see me. Within half an hour he was in my living room. 'Sam, I'm so sorry but you did break your leg when you fell last week.' He explained that the doctor who had originally assessed me had missed the break — probably at least in part because my leg didn't look much like a leg anymore.

At one stage there were 21 screws, three plates and two rods holding my bones together. I would have to go back to hospital immediately and I'd have to stay for at least another couple of weeks, maybe even up to a month, as it was likely I would need a couple of operations to fix it. 'Look,' he said, 'I've cleared my diary. You're coming in first thing in the morning for us to do this operation.' There was nothing I could say.

I tried to think of all the positive things that were going on in my life at the time. My amazing kids' lives, my beautiful wife's kisses, financial security, even the basics like a roof over our heads, food on the table. Thinking about this boosted my energy and attitude.

This episode really threw me but it also reminded me that crisis is messy and unpredictable and usually includes a number of curve balls. More often than not, just when you think you are making progress you will encounter a speed hump or someone will throw a dirty great spanner into the mix, which can so easily push you back and grind down your resilience and perseverance. Don't allow nasty surprises to derail you; change is never a linear process.

## Embrace the change process

Crisis by definition implies a period of uncertainty and change. If you want to successfully bounce forward into a better future following a crisis or challenge, then you will probably have to alter your behaviour in some way.

Hundreds of years ago Goethe wrote, 'Progress has not followed a straight ascending line, but a spiral with rhythms of progress and retrogression, of evolution and dissolution.' More recently three behavioural scientists, James Prochaska, John Norcross and Carlo Diclemente, explored this idea further in their book *Changing for Good*. These scientists reviewed every major change methodology and agreed with Goethe's insight that behavioural change is spiral rather than linear in nature. Crisis or extreme challenge is usually an invitation or warning to change, and that change process is not straightforward. Instead you will spiral through phases of progress and failure. After my initial crisis, the car accident, I worked my tail off to make progress, and I assumed that I would just keep getting better and better in an upward, linear progression. As I lay on my back on that freezing June morning, looking up at the grey sky, I was reminded that often crisis feels more like three steps forward and two steps back. Progress is almost always followed by a faltering, stagnation or a backslide.

In those trying times we assume that we are failing or that the change we are trying to implement won't work, and we can so easily get disheartened. But it is just the normal, expected process of change. Accept that, embrace it and move forward, even if the forward momentum feels negligible at times. When you hit the speed bumps, celebrate because it is evidence that you have been making progress, and leverage that positivity to fuel additional success as you spiral upward.

## Habits: Leverage positivity to fuel success

To ensure that you successfully emerge from crisis or difficulty, you need to gather positive momentum through the transition period. In short, you need to foster the following habits:

1. Take a stand and stay in motion.

2. Foster optimism.

3. Live a grateful life.

4. Celebrate wins.

# 1 TAKE A STAND AND STAY IN MOTION

At first sight you may think this sounds contradictory. After all, taking a stand implies that you stand still and become rooted to a position, which is the opposite of staying in motion. But both are necessary. Sooner or later in every crisis you will need to make a decision and take a stand in relation to what is happening to you.

The word 'decide' comes from the Latin *decidere*, which literally means to cut off from. A true decision therefore is not based on a whim or a notion; it's when you take a stand and cut yourself off from any other position. Obviously, in business and life you need to maintain some flexibility about strategy and tactics, but you do not need the same flexibility around your outlook and attitude.

When I first went to hospital it was soon pretty clear that my right leg was never going to be the same again, regardless of how many operations they performed on it. I still remember the day when the doctor told me that I probably wouldn't walk again. I was watching him talk to me, I could see his lips moving so I knew he was talking to me, but I'd stopped listening at 'you'll never walk again'. My mind quickly filled in the blanks: If I wasn't going to walk then I wasn't going to be able to play basketball anymore. I wouldn't be able to take part in the theatre activities I loved so much, I wouldn't be able to dance anymore. Worst of all, I would never be able to walk my daughters down the aisle.

It was also pretty obvious by that point that I'd lost my right arm so I wasn't going to be able to play the guitar again either. My right arm was my dominant arm so I'd have to relearn everything — how to write with my left hand, how to feed myself and how to use a prosthetic limb. It felt like my world had shrunk overnight. So many of the things I took for granted were now going to be really difficult, if not impossible. And I must admit I was pretty blue about it all, until someone said something to me that changed my outlook forever: 'Sam, it is your decision not your condition that determines who you are.'

I was stunned. That simple statement resonated so deeply within me that I resolved then and there that I would not accept the doctor's prognosis. I was going to take a stand and stay in motion. My friend was right. Sure, things did not look very good for me, but no-one — not even the doctors — knew for sure what my future held. We can't always control what happens to us, but we can always control what we decide those events and situations mean. It is the meaning we give events that can cause the real problems, not the situations themselves. By now Kate and I were old hands at defying medical prognoses and I was sure I could rustle up another miracle if I just believed I could.

Like most couples, when we first married we just assumed we'd have a family but after two and a half years' trying Kate was still not pregnant. Eventually, after a battery of tests, scans and hormone injections and countless examinations, Kate was told by her doctor that her body didn't ovulate on its own and as a result she had 'unexplained infertility'. She was put on a medication that would hopefully trigger ovulation, and once her body started to ovulate properly then hopefully everything would work out. We were pretty devastated by the news — especially Kate. Her 'why' in life had always been to have a family and she had long dreamed of being a mother. But the medication didn't work, so they increased the dose and we were told that if this didn't work then the only option open to us would be IVF. So when the increased dosage still didn't work we were lost for words. At the time there was no way we could afford IVF.

Like me, Kate was brought up in a religious family and certainly her faith was strongly tested during this period. One day when she was feeling particularly upset she decided to play 'Bible Bingo', a game her mother had taught her when she was a little girl. It sounds a little irreverent but basically when she needed answers or guidance her mum told her to close her eyes, open the bible at a random page and let her finger trace down the page until she felt like she'd arrived at the right spot, then open her eyes and read what the Bible said. Sitting in our living room sobbing, Kate took down the Bible from the bookshelf and did as her mum had instructed years earlier. When she opened her eyes her finger had stopped at 'He settles the barren woman in her home as a joyful mother of children'.

Whether you believe in God or not is irrelevant to this story, although our belief is deeply relevant to us. The critical point is that we believed this was a sign that we would have a family. Was it coincidence? Was it luck? Was it God? Who knows? But we knew what we believe and that belief fuelled us and lifted Kate's sadness. She stopped seeing the doctor because she knew there was nothing more he could do. She was told to contact him if anything changed. Two weeks later she called to explain that her period was two weeks late, so she went in for tests. The next day her doctor called: 'Hi Kate, are you sitting down? I don't know how to explain it, but congratulations — you're pregnant!' We were over the moon. I think my first reaction was, 'Oh my goodness, we're going to be parents!' I was just so shocked after we'd been told we would never have children naturally.

No-one knows the future, not even doctors, so when my doctor told me I wasn't going to walk again I remembered Kate and our lovely little family. I knew that my prognosis wasn't great but it was certainly not going to be improved by my slipping into melancholy and depression. I needed a plan and I needed to get into motion and stay in motion. I needed to cut myself off completely from the possibility that I wouldn't walk again. I refused to accept it and moved confidently in the other direction, and you can do the same regardless of the challenges you face.

I knew the doctors were just trying to be realistic and get me to accept what had happened, but I was going to take a stand and prove them wrong or die trying!

No-one knows what the future will hold and sometimes life dishes up some cruel blows. Whether, like me, you have suffered a physical injury, disfigurement or illness, or the crisis you face is professional, you need to take a stand and choose to stay positive and seek a solution.

The world was shocked at the news that *Superman* actor Christopher Reeve was paralysed from the neck down following a freak riding accident. He was just 43 years old at the time. Reeve had two options: he could allow the accident to define him and become consumed in bitterness and self-pity or he could decide that it wouldn't. He chose the latter. In an interview Reeve said, 'You play the hand you're dealt. I think the game's worthwhile.' His game certainly changed that day, but he took a stand. He used his influence and status to further spinal injury research and became an outspoken advocate of stem cell research, which he believed held the solution for thousands of people with similar injuries.

Christopher Reeve may have acted the role of Superman on the big screen but it was his decisions and actions after suffering a tragic personal crisis that elevated him to the ranks of real superhero. Or, as he reminded us, 'I think a hero is an ordinary individual who finds the strength to persevere and endure in spite of overwhelming obstacles. They are the real heroes, and so are the families and friends who have stood by them.'

Bad stuff happens to good people. Stock markets crash, mergers fall apart and businesses lose major accounts, relationships break down and people are diagnosed with life-altering illnesses or experience random accidents that alter the course of their life. But positivity is always still a choice. It is our decisions not our conditions that determine who we are and what we are capable of. Based on their knowledge and expertise, the doctors thought I would not walk again, but they didn't take account of my attitude and my determination to prove them wrong.

Whatever your crisis or difficulty there will come a time when you have to put a stake in the ground, decide on the future and just go for it. You need to banish negativity and doubt and just keep putting one foot in front of the other. You need to take a stand, take action and stay in motion.

Instead of focusing my attention on all the things I couldn't do or might never be able to do, I focused on what I could still do. I took pleasure in the little wins.

Another powerful moment of overcoming other people's expectations for me was when the doctors explained how and why I'd lost my dominant arm. One implication was clear: I would never play the guitar again. I had been playing the guitar since I was seven years old. I played most days. It was an emotional and mental release for me at the end of a busy day, and it made me happy. To me there was something spiritual about playing; it was just part of my nature and character. I couldn't imagine not being able to access that joy. So when the doctors said that I would probably never play again, it was devastating but again I was determined to prove them wrong.

A few months after my accident some friends of mine found a woman in Canada with an above-elbow amputation who plays the guitar. So we made contact with her and she gave me hope that it was possible. She kindly provided me with the details of the person who made her prosthetic 'guitar arm', who in turn contacted my designer. It took a few frustrating months to engineer something that was going to work, but eventually we created a guitar prosthetic. It was an amazing achievement and I was overjoyed — not just because I could play again but also because I'd successfully conquered another major hurdle — and I was deeply grateful to everyone involved.

Goethe put it best when he said, 'Whatever you can do, or dream you can, begin it. Boldness has genius, power, and magic in it!'

Scottish mountaineer W. H. Murray expanded on Goethe's original insight in an equally famous quote:

**Until one is committed, there is hesitancy, the chance to draw back, always ineffectiveness. Concerning all acts of initiative and creation there is one elementary truth, the ignorance of which kills countless ideas and splendid plans: that the moment one definitely commits oneself, then providence moves too. All sorts of things occur to help one that would never otherwise have occurred. A whole stream of events issue from the decision, raising in one's favour all manner of unforeseen incidents and meetings and material assistance which no man could have dreamed would have come his way.**

The magic that Goethe refers to and Murray alludes to is accessible only when you take a stand, turn away from the alternatives and get into positive action. And sometimes that requires a leap of faith.

An exercise I regularly do in my seminars demonstrates to participants that happiness is ignited by motion. In the first part of the exercise I ask everyone to stand up, walk around the room and introduce themselves to everyone else. They are to pretend they are in a bad mood and don't care about the exercise or the other people at all. Interestingly, most people do this exercise with their heads down, shoulders slumped, making minimal eye contact, even though that wasn't part of the instructions. There is also not much physical touch, and if people do shake hands it's a small, weak gesture.

I then ask the group to stop and do exactly the opposite. This time they are to introduce themselves enthusiastically. They are to be excited and over the top. Again almost everyone in the room already knows how to do this and they will immediately lift their heads, push back their shoulders and make direct eye contact while vigorously shaking hands with or hugging their neighbours. Again I didn't tell them to do that — it's just the universally understood language of enthusiastic contact. From this simple exercise everyone realises the powerful impact of our physiology and that happiness and positivity are initially generated and inspired by our physiology. The way we choose to use our body determines how we show up in life. Happiness is ignited by motion.

## Start bouncing

### Choose the meaning

Take a moment to think about your current crisis or challenge. Chances are you won't be able to think of much else anyway so this task should be easy. What are you making this situation mean in your head? Think about emotions and feelings as well as scenarios you are anticipating because of the situation. What have you already imagined could happen as a result of this situation?

It's important for you to be able to separate the crisis — the facts of what is actually happening — from the meaning you have ascribed to these events. Events don't destroy people; it is the meaning that destroys people.

## 2 FOSTER OPTIMISM

Most people have heard about the importance of optimism. People talk about whether someone's glass is half full or half empty. In other words, when the normal ups and downs of life occur is your natural disposition toward positivity or negativity?

One of the big questions around this topic is whether optimism is determined by nature or nurture. Are we born with a particular level of positivity or is it conditioned in us, or is it a combination of both? To shine some light on this question David Lykken, a researcher from the University of Minnesota, gathered information on 4000 sets of twins. In the study he compared happiness and positivity between twins, including twins separated at birth, and he concluded that 50 percent of your innate positivity is determined by your genetic disposition, 8 percent is shaped by circumstantial factors such as income, marital status and education, and the remaining 42 percent can be put down to 'life's slings and arrows'. In other words, whether you see your glass as half empty or half full depends to a greater or lesser extent on your genes, your environment, your conditioning and the experiences you have in your life.

For many years it was assumed that this characteristic was pretty fixed. So if you didn't hit the genetic positivity jackpot when you were born, then you were pretty much assigned to a half-empty outlook. Luckily for us, psychologist Dr Martin Seligman disagreed. Prior to Seligman the field of psychology was interested only in studying and treating dysfunction. Professionals were almost solely focused on what could go wrong for a person and how to get them back to an optimal psychological level. Seligman was curious about the other side of the coin. He has dedicated his career to understanding positive psychology — the study of human wellbeing rather than illness. A psychology professor and director of the positive

Psychology Center at the University of Pennsylvania, Seligman was also elected as president of the American Psychological Association by the widest margin in the association's history. Seligman is the thirteenth most frequently cited psychologist this century.

His mission was to unpack what made optimists optimistic so the insights could help others who were not born optimistic or whose life experiences had worn down their inherent optimism to live better, happier and more productive lives. In his book *Learned Optimism* Seligman states, 'Literally hundreds of studies show that pessimists give up more easily and get depressed more often. These experiments show that optimists do much better in school and college, at work and on the playing field.'

This theory, known as *learned helplessness*, suggests that pessimism is mainly learned and therefore something more constructive can be adopted in its place. When crisis hits your life, your ability to rise to the challenge and bounce into a better life will be significantly influenced by your ability to demonstrate optimism. And if that isn't your natural set point don't worry, because optimism can be taught.

Think of optimism and pessimism as a temperature range. At one end you have 'Negative Norman'. Norman is operating at freezing. Every second day he thinks the world is about to end. Nothing good ever happens. Life just sucks and then you die. He's not much fun at parties! At the other end of the spectrum is 'Positive Pollyanna'. Pollyanna is operating at 35 degrees all the time. She'd still be rosy in the middle of a tornado and can find a silver lining in absolutely *anything*. What we now know, however, is that Negative Norman and Positive Pollyanna are not locked into one outlook; instead they operate within a range. So even if you naturally lean more toward pessimism than optimism you actually fluctuate across a range. And once you understand the component parts of optimism you can actively take control of that range so that you consistently operate at a higher or optimistic level.

Those component parts are what Seligman calls your 'explanatory style'. As the name would suggest, your explanatory style identifies how you explain events and situations to yourself and others. The building blocks of explanatory style are:

» permanence

» pervasiveness

» personalisation.

### Permanence

When you are faced with a serious challenge or crisis, what level of permanence do you assume around the event? It has been found that pessimists have a tendency to view these situations as permanent and will use words such as 'always' ('This stuff *always* happens to me') or 'never' ('I can *never* catch a break') or 'everything' ('*Everything* always goes wrong') as a way of extending the life of the challenge. Or as Seligman says, 'People who give up easily believe the causes of the bad events that happen to them are permanent.'

Often these events are assumed to stem from a personal defect that will have permanent repercussions in that person's life. On that basis it's pretty easy to become helpless and feel that nothing you do will matter.

Optimists, on the other hand, see events and situations as temporary. Even in the midst of crisis these people believe all things will pass and tomorrow will be a brighter day. Just because something unpleasant is happening now does not resign that person to a life of distress.

## Pervasiveness

The second component of optimism and pessimism relates to scope or how far the challenge disseminates across other areas of a person's life.

A pessimist will experience a negative effect or situation and automatically assume that the situation in one area will pollute every other area of his or her life. A missed train, failed exam or winter cold is assumed to affect all areas of their life, not just the ones that are directly involved in their descent into negativity. The misfortune is therefore allowed to spread its negativity to corrupt other perfectly functional areas of life. Any positive situations that occur during this time will be ignored or discounted as unimportant.

An optimist sees things very differently. Optimists are much better at seeing negative situations or circumstances as isolated incidents whose effects are limited. The negativity isn't amplified or energised and it does not go on to pollute other areas.

As Seligman points out, 'People who make *universal* explanations for their failures give up on everything when a failure strikes in one area. People who make *specific* explanations may become helpless in that one part of their lives yet march stalwartly on in the others.'

## Personalisation

The final component you will need to master to increase your optimism levels is personalisation. Seligman found there are essentially two choices: you can either internalise the blame or externalise the blame.

A pessimist's natural response is to internalise the blame and assume that the crisis is their fault. They will therefore make the situation or negative event personal. Strangely enough, when things go right for a pessimist they are much more likely to externalise the situation and assume that this random piece of good fortune had absolutely nothing to do with them personally! So a pessimist will blame themselves for negativity and attribute success to others.

The optimist is the exact opposite. When things go badly for an optimist they will assume it was because of external events over which they had no control. If things go well then they will be happy to take the credit! Seligman states, 'The optimistic style of explaining good events is the opposite of that used for bad events; it's internal rather than external. People who believe they cause good things tend to like themselves better than people who believe good things come from other people or circumstances.' It's therefore logical that people who like themselves better are happier, more productive, more creative and more sociable. And those traits tend to multiply themselves and attract more good things into the mix.

Without conscious intervention to actively foster the habit of optimism your explanatory style won't change that much. This was proven fairly dramatically when Seligman interviewed the Harvard graduating class of 1939–44 and then followed their progress at five-year intervals following their return from the Second World War. Seligman reported, 'The men's explanatory style at age 25 predicted their health at 65. Around age 45 the health of the pessimists started to deteriorate more quickly.'

Nothing positive — and I mean *nothing* positive — can come from negativity in a crisis. In a crisis you need access to energy, action, confidence, self-esteem, enthusiasm and creativity, and all those things are extinguished by pessimism.

Optimism is not the elixir that will solve every crisis but it is an essential ingredient. By taking control of this aspect of your nature and getting into the habit of viewing setbacks and challenges as temporary, isolated and external, you can successfully make the transition out of crisis in the minimum amount of time.

Pessimists (or realists) may get things right more often than optimists because they see the world in its current form, but optimists see the world as it could be and sculpt their experiences to mirror their imagination. Only the optimists can change the world.

Your explanatory style is the key to fostering optimism and tapping into your very best every day. Burying your head in the sand or trying to point fingers of blame and recrimination is useless as a strategy moving forward. And from that standpoint optimists can be every bit as delusional as pessimists, but optimism is an essential part of finding a constructive solution so we must learn to take greater control over what bumps us on and off course.

If you are thinking explanatory style is a little woolly and does not relate to business, think again. Seligman was retained by insurance giant MetLife to see if he could help with sales and agent turnover. What he discovered was that salespeople with an optimistic explanatory style outsold the rest by 37 percent and that the most optimistic style sold 88 percent more than the most pessimistic. Furthermore those with an optimistic explanatory style were half as likely to leave the job. Based on these findings MetLife hired a new group of agents based only on their explanatory style. Within two years that group had outperformed their most pessimistic counterparts by a whopping 57 percent. MetLife have since switched their entire recruitment process to a focus on explanatory style. The result? Agent turnover has dropped dramatically and market share has increased by 50 percent.

**TWIXT THE OPTIMIST AND PESSIMIST
THE DIFFERENCE IS DROLL
THE OPTIMIST SEES THE DOUGHNUT
BUT THE PESSIMIST SEES THE HOLE.**

**– MCLANDBURGH WILSON**

# Start bouncing

### Expose your explanatory style

Take a moment to consider the situation you are currently in. You've already identified what meanings you have ascribed to this situation so this exercise should be an easy next step. Be honest . . .

*Permanent:* Do you feel that the situation is permanent or that it will happen again so it doesn't matter what you do, or do you see it as a temporary issue for which you need to find a solution?

*Pervasive:* Do you feel that the challenge or situation is corrupting your whole life, or are you able to segment the situation and stop it from spilling into other important areas of your life?

*Personal:* Do you believe that you are to blame for this situation, even if you would never admit it to anyone, or do you feel the crisis was caused by an external issue?

If this exercise highlights that your explanatory style is more pessimistic than optimistic, go back through each

*(Continued)*

97

> ## Start bouncing *(Cont'd)*
>
> question and actively shift your mindset to reframe the crisis you are experiencing as temporary, isolated and external.

## 3 LIVE A GRATEFUL LIFE

Sometimes things just don't go according to plan.

In January 2005 my younger brother David was diagnosed with acute lymphoblastic leukemia. He'd not been feeling great for months and eventually went for tests, and that's when they discovered the cancer. He was only 19 years old.

David had radiation treatment and chemotherapy, and it was terrible watching him lose his hair and become weaker and weaker but we all believed he would beat it. Initially the treatment was successful and David went into remission, but by 2006 it came back and it was clear that his leukemia was no longer responding to treatment. The only way he would survive was through a bone marrow transplant. Bone marrow is not like a blood transfusion — you have to find someone who is an exact match and it is a very painful procedure for the donor. The best chance of finding a match is to test all the immediate family members, so the whole Cawthorn family stepped forward. When the results came back there were only two matches — me and my older brother Tim. At the time Tim was going through his own tough times so I volunteered to be the donor. I flew to the Bone Marrow Institute in Melbourne with David. By this point he was very sick and couldn't stand for long. I remember lying on the bed as they were taking the bone marrow — which is indeed excruciatingly painful — and David came up to me, crutch under one arm, the other arm holding on to his drip, and he put his hand gently on my shoulder and we just looked at each other in silence. I knew how grateful he was that I was helping him and the pain eased away as we looked at each other.

The great news is that the bone marrow transplant was successful. David's leukemia again went into remission and we were over the moon. It felt like a weight had been lifted from the whole family and we could all start to look forward to the future again. Then a few weeks later I had my accident. When Kate called my mum she was with David at the Bone Marrow Institute and the two of them caught a plane to Tasmania immediately. I can't imagine how hard that must have been for my parents. By this point they had been helping David fight his cancer for over a year, caring for him and supporting him through his treatment, and just when things started to look better for David I had my car accident. Mum didn't even recognise me when she saw me the first time lying in the intensive care unit.

There were funny times too, though — David and I comparing notes and arguing about which condition was the most life-threatening. We'd always been competitive! We'd also always been close, but we became even closer through the bone marrow treatment and he would visit me often during my recovery. He was my best friend.

But our luck didn't hold. In June 2008 I broke my leg again and we were told that David's leukemia had come back with a vengeance and he had about six weeks to live. Kate and I visited as often as we could, although by this time Kate was heavily pregnant with our third child and my own recovery had been put back by my slip on the ice. To add to our grief my dad, Peter, suffered a heart attack and was also in hospital. It was an extremely difficult time. Losing David at the same time as we were getting ready to welcome a new member of the Cawthorn family seemed bittersweet for all of us and emotions were running high.

Thankfully Dad made a full recovery but David died on 16 July 2008. I can honestly say that losing him was far worse than losing my arm. Death is a strange thing; even when you are expecting it and you know it's coming it's still a shock. We all believed that he was going to make it — even toward the end. He'd successfully defied the six-week prediction and we took comfort from that. My parents took it especially hard. No parent should ever outlive their own children, and I think they blamed themselves in some way that perhaps their faith hadn't been strong enough. But no matter how much we hope or pray, things don't always go according to plan. It's like we assume terrible things just happen to 'other people' and that somehow our family or our business or our friends will be immune to the randomness and unfairness of life.

You may be wondering what this story has to do with living a grateful life, but David taught me to be grateful for the time he was here. He reminded me just how precious and wonderful life can be — even the horrible bits. He may not be with us anymore but we enjoyed 21 years together. We laughed and we fought, we fell out and made up and laughed some more. I would have preferred longer but we owe it to ourselves and the people left behind to be grateful for the time we have.

To this day I am sad that David is no longer with us, but his memory reminds me every day to celebrate what I do have. It's not just injury that can bring people down; stress, loneliness, failure, pressure and isolation can do it too. Thinking about how things have gone wrong in your life can be really disheartening but you need to learn how to snap yourself out of it, count your blessings and move forward. Be grateful and make the change. It doesn't matter that I've lost my arm or my leg doesn't work. I know in my heart that I am blessed. I still have the most amazing wife and kids — we welcomed our son Jacob 'David' Cawthorn into our family less than a month after David died. My kids love me unconditionally, no matter what. This is my reality check. None of us can afford to take life for granted. You are alive today for a reason and a purpose. I'm alive today for a reason and a purpose, and I no longer take a moment of that for granted. I enjoy an amazing life, I love what I do and I love having the opportunity to help others find their own way through crisis.

When you foster an attitude of gratitude you open yourself up to more positivity, which in turn fuels success. At the University of California psychologist Sonja Lyubomirsky has studied the best ways to boost positivity and happiness, and gratitude is a real winner. Simply by taking the time to consciously count your blessings — even once every week — will increase your satisfaction and happiness levels. Psychologist Robert Emmons from the same university also found that gratitude improved physical health, raising energy levels and relieving pain and fatigue. What's more, he discovered, 'The ones who benefit most tended to elaborate more and have a wider span of things they're grateful for.'

## Start bouncing

### *Keep a gratitude journal*

Start a gratitude diary. Every week write down all the things in your life that you are currently grateful for. If you need an extra boost of energy then try this every day. If your crisis is professional, then get your team together and brainstorm all the things you are grateful for right now. Celebrate the clients you have already, look at the positive feedback you've already got from happy customers, remind yourselves of all the ways in which you are already succeeding and use that positivity to fuel further success.

*(Continued)*

> ## Start bouncing (Cont'd)
>
> Rather than getting worked up and frustrated by your daily commute to and from work, use the time to connect to the things you are already grateful for in your life. Record them on your mobile phone or just list them all to yourself every morning and every night. I challenge you to do this for just seven days — it will transform your mindset.
>
> Once you've exhausted your list of things you are grateful for consider finishing with a little song I often sing to myself: 'I am blessed, I am blessed, every day of my life I am blessed. When I wake up in the morning and lay my head to rest I am blessed, I am blessed.'

## 4 CELEBRATE WINS

You'll have heard this one before but do you do it?

When was the last time you complimented your partner or told your kids you were proud of them for something — even something little such as cleaning their room without being nagged? Often it is the little things that bind people together in the first place.

When was the last time you congratulated a member of your team or another manager on a job well done? When was the last time you took a moment to stop and appreciate what you and your team have collectively achieved?

Considering how infrequently we encourage, congratulate and compliment others in the normal course of daily life, it's safe to assume that during a crisis celebrating wins becomes one of the last things you feel like doing.

The big problem when it comes to acknowledging ourselves and others for what we've achieved so far is that we keep raising the bar. In business we are expected to keep improving to maintain and increase shareholder value. As a result, even if things are going well and we achieve a target there is rarely any joy in that accomplishment. Instead the target is increased and we set off to chase the new target without so much as a pat on the back or a glimmer of glory. So what we should be celebrating becomes expected and commonplace and it's never considered good enough.

Also, certainly in business, many managers and leaders don't want to be seen to praise their people in case they then turn around and ask for a pay rise! The assumption is that if someone is doing well and the manager acknowledges that, there will come a time when that person will demand a tangible reward for that effort, whereas if the manager says nothing then this won't happen and the business will save money.

For centuries academics and scientists believed that there were only two motivational drives. They believed people did things for one of only two reasons: survival or to gain reward, and avoid punishment. The biological imperative is an intrinsic motivation, meaning it comes from within and relates to our drive to survive. We are capable of amazing things — good and bad — when our survival is threatened. The second motivational drive is reward or punishment. These are extrinsic motivations, meaning the impetus for action comes from an external source. Business has long assumed that the best way to get staff to follow through and meet a deadline is to reward them when they do or threaten redundancy if they don't. And it is this misunderstanding that helps managers and leaders to justify the lack of celebration in their teams.

In his fascinating book *Drive: The Surprising Truth about What Motivates Us*, Daniel Pink provides compelling examples of the ineffectiveness of reward and punishment in a business setting. For example, when motivation expert Edward Deci, professor of psychology and Gowen Professor in the social sciences at the University of Rochester, and two colleagues reviewed 30 years of research to assess 128 experiments on motivation they concluded that 'tangible rewards tend to have a substantially negative effect on intrinsic motivation'. The long-term damage caused by offering short-term tangible rewards is one of the most robustly proven findings in social science and yet it is constantly ignored.

For example, the US Federal Reserve commissioned research into the effectiveness of rewards on performance. The study concluded, 'In eight of the nine tasks we examined across three experiments, higher incentives led to worse performance.' This was confirmed by an analysis of 51 studies of corporate reward schemes undertaken by the London School of Economics. The researchers reported, 'We find that financial incentives . . . can result in negative impact on overall performance.'

Tangible reward and punishment don't work that well when you are interested in lifting morale and performance, but praise and public recognition for a job well done does lift performance. It also has positive effects on productivity and morale. And if that is true in the normal course of business then it's absolutely true in a crisis.

Celebrate the wins, regardless of how small. Take time out to speak to your people and acknowledge their contribution and you may be surprised by just how quickly you can turn things around and find solutions to the challenges you face.

The constant raising of the bar means we are in a state of perpetual discontent. Nothing is ever good enough so no achievement, however big, is ever celebrated. And that is a huge error whether your crisis is personal or professional.

I live by the philosophy that I am content but never satisfied. I'm content with the roof over my head, the food in my belly, my wife and my kids, but I'm still not satisfied. I want to achieve more, but that isn't bound up in my sense of self-worth or enjoyment of life. I love my work and I am incredibly grateful to have people in my life who support me no matter what. Perhaps if we all acknowledged and learned how to be grateful for what we already have, then there would be less depression in the world. Certainly I've found that it's difficult to be depressed and grateful at the same time.

Whatever you are experiencing right now, take time out to connect to friends and family. I'm lucky enough to be extremely busy with corporate training events, speaking and my foundation work, and I don't often have the time for these connections, but I make the time because I love just hanging out, having some fun, laughing with my friends and enjoying a beer. We think these interactions are frivolous and unnecessary, but they are the glue that hold us together — especially in difficult times.

Even in a pressure cooker environment such as Harvard students succeed or fail not just because of their academic ability but because of their willingness to make and maintain friendships. In his book *The Happiness Advantage* Shawn Achor tells the story of two Harvard roommates who chose different survival tactics. Stressed and overwhelmed by the workload, Amanda withdrew, severed contacts, ate alone and immersed herself in study. Brittney was also aware of the stress and workload but she took the opposite approach. She reached out and created study groups that would convene over lunch to discuss what everyone had found as well as catch up on personal news, and she would take time out from study to join activities like Oreo-eating contests! So what happened? Amanda dropped out and Brittney flourished because the work was made easier and more enjoyable by involving others and pooling resources.

## Start bouncing

### Make someone happy

If you are unaccustomed to dishing out compliments, it might help if you had some ground rules to work with. When you are giving feedback to others:

*Be specific.* Giving praise without detail feels fake to you and the person receiving it, so be specific about what you are celebrating or acknowledging. Praise effort and attitude as well as results so that you help others to foster a growth mindset.

*Focus on repeatable skills.* Praise what you want more of and actions that someone can do something about.

*Maintain a 3:1 positive to negative ratio.* Obviously not all feedback is going to be good, but try wherever possible to make three positive comments for every negative one you have to deliver.

In relation to your current situation or crisis think of three people who you need to acknowledge for their effort and input. Do it by the end of the day.

# How to ensure that you leverage positivity to fuel success

When you find yourself in the middle of a crisis the road ahead can seem long and lonely. The loneliness part can be solved pretty easily when you adhere to the Proximity is Power principle (refer to chapter 2) and foster the habits that will maintain your connections, stay in communication, and invest time and energy in the people around you. Sometimes there really is nothing much you can do about the long part. The transition through a crisis is a journey so it's essential to generate positivity and leverage it moving forward.

My life as a professional speaker has its benefits but also its tough times. I regularly make more than 30 flights a month both internationally and domestic, and being 6 foot 3 inches tall and living with a right leg that doesn't bend makes flying particularly difficult.

I occasionally fly business class but I mainly travel economy, and even in business my leg can get very painful in a chair designed for people who are shorter and have two legs that bend! Initially I used to take strong pain medication and when I got to the destination I would rest for 24 hours. Today I take no pain medication but I use my positive personality and negotiation skills to try to secure a seat that will allow me to be more comfortable. I then use my positive energy and thoughts to minimise the pain during the flight. So instead of getting upset about it I make sure I get up and move around, drink lots of fluids, do muscle exercises and focus on the adventures that await me when I get off the flight, whether that's returning to my family or a new opportunity to talk to people about the power of bounce. That way, regardless of the pain and the punishing schedule, I enjoy every flight and look at ways that I can have a positive experience each time I fly so I arrive at my destination excited about what lies ahead.

Below is the A.B.C. for ensuring that you leverage positivity to fuel success:

*Appreciate.* Practise being appreciative of all that you have, whether it is a little or a lot. Appreciation is an incredibly powerful emotion that can help you to stay positive by frequently reminding you how lucky you already are. We get so used to our life as we live it that we take for granted some of the most precious gifts we have, such as our loved ones, health and peace of mind. An appreciative heart is good medicine that should be taken at least once every day.

*Believe.* Believe in yourself and life. Tough times don't last but tough people do. No matter how bleak things look today the sun will rise tomorrow; tomorrow is a brand-new day, so practise believing in a positive outcome. We don't always see the big picture and sometimes difficult times are necessary to get us to a better, happier and more productive place. There is a saying that everything works out in the end and if it hasn't worked out then it's just not the end. Believing the best in others and that it will all work out for the best creates an optimistic and healthy attitude, which can help to facilitate that result.

*Cheerful.* Life isn't always a bed of roses. As adults we have to take the good with the bad, but practising cheerfulness and being lighthearted will always make things better. Whether in a crisis, a tough time or even a trauma, a lighthearted approach can not only help you but help all the people around you too. I'm not suggesting you don't take your challenges seriously —

just not too seriously, because by drawing on the lighter side of life you can inspire others through your example.

Microsoft is a classic example of what's possible with some self-belief, a bold vision and buckets of positivity. It is still one of the largest and most successful businesses of all time and yet it started in 1975 during a period of economic difficulty.

The only working computers in 1975 were massive, room-sized machines that cost millions of dollars and required specialist programmers to operate, but Microsoft founders Bill Gates and Paul Allen believed that the day would come when every home would have a computer, and they were going to put it there.

The story behind Microsoft is well known but worth repeating as a demonstration of what's possible with positivity and a 'never say die' attitude. Allen and Gates had been high-school friends and Allen was on his way to meet Gates at Harvard when he picked up a copy of *Popular Electronics*. On the cover was a picture of the Altair 8800 under the headline, 'World's First Microcomputer Kit to Rival Commercial Models'. Convinced that the computer market was going to explode, making them accessible to everyone, this article indicated a start to that process and Gates wanted in. He called Micro Instrumentation and Telemetry Systems (MITS), the makers of the Altair, and told them that he and Allen had developed a BASIC programming language that could be used on the Altair. Obviously, MITS wanted to see it and the pair scheduled a meeting several weeks later.

This then gave them the time they needed to develop the software they had convinced MITS they already had. In reality, neither Gates nor Allen had written a single line of code and they hadn't even seen an Altair in the flesh!

History will attest that the meeting went well, despite the fact that they had never tested the program on an Altair machine. MITS arranged a deal with Gates and Allen and Microsoft was on its way to being the technological giant it is today. Through perseverance and positivity they changed the computer industry forever and made significant inroads in putting a computer on every desk.

## The big picture: Positivity is a decision

Regardless of your natural positivity range, being a positive person and using that to help you through a crisis or difficult time is fundamentally a choice.

The stuff and circumstances of life don't really affect happiness and fulfilment. That much has already been proven by science. We know, for example, that people who win the lottery are happy for a short period of time, then they will normalise. It is the contrast that supplies the initial buzz, but once that contrast diminishes and the individual gets used to their new wealth they will normally return to their natural set point. In the same way, when someone suffers a terrible injury, such as the type experienced by actor Christopher Reeve, they too will normalise in time and return to close to their natural set point.

Today there is a huge body of knowledge on positive psychology. We now know what contributes to happiness and positive wellbeing, and it's not what we had imagined. Happiness does not, for example, depend on money. Of course not having enough money can have a marked influence on happiness, but what is enough? Researchers from Princeton University decided to find out by studying Gallup data for almost half a million Americans. It turns out that 'enough' is around $75000. Once this magical threshold had been reached all the benefits of having more money appeared to taper off entirely.

We assume money will make us happier and more positive, but all the evidence suggests it won't. In another experiment, Elizabeth Dunn, an associate professor of psychology at the University of British Columbia, and Michael Norton, an associate professor of business administration at Harvard Business School, took a national sample of Americans who earned around $25 000. All respondents reported that they thought their satisfaction with life would double if they made $55000. So Dunn and Norton took another national sample of people who already earned $55000 to assess whether they were twice as happy as those living on $25 000. They were not. Those on $55 000 were actually only 9 percent happier than those who made $25 000.

Gaining a great education doesn't help much either in the happiness and positivity stakes. Neither does living in a pleasant climate. According to psychologist Dr Martin Seligman, what really matters is satisfying work, avoiding negative events as much as possible, being married and having strong social networks. If you also demonstrate gratitude, optimism and forgiveness, then you will live a life full of positive emotions about your past, present and future — you will have what Seligman refers to as a 'pleasant life'.

To move beyond a pleasant life to a 'good life', you need to use your 'signature strengths' in the main area of your life, which is usually your work. In other words, you have to work out what you are especially good at and do that more often. We'll discuss this idea in more detail in chapter 5. If you can achieve this, then your work moves from the 'daily grind' to a 'calling'. Making sure that everyone in your team is aligned to their 'signature strengths' is also great for business, as it will increase productivity and profitability.

To move beyond a 'good life', you need to develop a 'life of meaning' in which you direct your signature strengths toward a purpose and cause bigger than you, your career or your business. A 'life of meaning' can really ignite positivity and fuel perpetual success. And meaning largely comes down to the decisions you make.

Human beings adapt, both to the very best of events and to the very worst. It is change that ignites the emotions and keeps us vibrant and fresh. And it is change and the decisions we make around whether that change is good or bad that allow us to recalibrate our natural set point. By fostering the habits identified in this chapter you can move yourself to the upper levels of your natural range and reinvent yourself whenever you need to.

# CHAPTER 4
# Principle 4: Bounce forward not back

After my accident I knew that what had happened to me couldn't be just a fluke. I couldn't be the only person in the world who had suffered a setback and used the experience to bounce forward. I knew fairly quickly that I didn't want to bounce back to my old life — I wanted something more. They say a brush with death will do that to a person!

It didn't seem right to me that when we were faced with the inevitable challenges of life we had only two options: we could let the challenge destroy us or diminish us in some way, or at best we could recover to a pre-crisis status quo. There had to be a third option. Many people have used adversity to propel them in a new, better direction, but these people are seen as special or unique in some way. It seemed to me that those individuals were revered but not researched; little effort was made to unpack the hallmarks of this third option. It was untouchable and out of reach to all but the chosen few. I wanted to change that.

I'm an ordinary guy. I don't have five degrees or letters after my name and I don't have money coming out of my ears, but I was able to bounce forward after my accident and the death of my brother, though I still miss him every day. And frankly, if I could do that then it isn't untouchable or out of reach — it's a legitimate third option for everyone facing difficult times.

So I became obsessed with bounce and specifically bouncing in the right direction! The more I thought about it, the clearer it became that the reason failure and setback disheartens people so much is that they focus all their efforts on getting back to where they were before the crisis rather than on creating a new and better future. As a result they lose their momentum, and once you lose your momentum it can be really difficult to get moving again. Early on in my recovery I realised that the main reason I was doing so well was because I was determined to move forward, to put my problems in the past and create a new life for myself and my family.

### THE FINEST STEEL GOES THROUGH THE HOTTEST FIRE.
### — RICHARD NIXON

On 3 October 2007, exactly a year after my accident, I held a big celebration. I wanted to mark the day and share it with all the people who had helped me achieve the impossible. After all I was told I wouldn't walk again so I had plenty to celebrate. I also wanted to use the event as a springboard to publicly announce my new direction.

About 120 people attended the event in Launceston, Tasmania, including close friends, relatives, and my doctors and nurses — I invited my whole rehabilitation team. The police officer who investigated my crash, the paramedics who got me to the hospital and my insurance representative were also there (I wanted to say a special thank you to my insurance company for financially supporting me and paying for the remodelling of my house). I even invited the truck driver whose truck I'd smashed into! These were the people who had, in one way or another, contributed to my realisation that my old life hadn't been working for me, and I wanted these same people to be the first to know the new direction I was bouncing into.

In the previous months I had started to tell more and more people about my accident. I was asked by my local pastor if I would address the congregation and tell everyone the story of my accident and recovery. I agreed so he advertised it in the local paper. Normally there were around fifty people at church but on that day hundreds packed in, eager to hear from the guy who'd been in that horrible accident on the Bass Highway. There were even people standing along the back wall.

I had expected the usual size of congregation so I was pretty surprised by the turnout. I hadn't really prepared anything so I just started telling the audience what had happened. This experience sparked something in me. I already knew that I didn't want my old life back, that I wanted more. And when I shared my story I could see how much it helped others to reconnect to the things that were important in their life. I made space for something new and better to enter my life, and it did. For whatever reason, my story resonated with people. I could see that my experiences helped them to gain a new perspective on whatever was happening in their own lives. I realised that we all have problems, but often the journey out of those challenges is lonely and poorly lit!

I knew that I wanted to dedicate my life to illuminating such difficulties so I could unpack the process of recovery and help others to bounce out of their own crises to a new, happier and more successful future. This was a perfect way for me to live my purpose of being caring, passionate and really making a difference in the world.

When I announced that day that I was going to bounce into a new career as a motivational speaker the audience erupted. It was an emotional event for everyone, and at the end of the night the insurance rep came up to me and whispered in my ear, 'Sam, I want you to send me the bill for tonight.' I couldn't believe it!

There I was thanking everyone for all the help and support they'd given me in getting me to that stage, and now I was being offered even more help.

# Habits: Bounce forward not back

Instead of focusing all your energy on regaining the old status quo, you need to refocus on bouncing forward into something better than before. The following four habits will make that process easier and easier over time:

1. Forget the past and press forward.
2. Expect the best.
3. Empower your strengths.
4. Stay aligned and motivated.

## 1 FORGET THE PAST AND PRESS FORWARD

The other day at a presentation I was doing on bounce I was speaking with a 45-year-old lady who told me that she hadn't spoken to her sister in 15 years. I asked her why not and she told me they'd had a fight. So I asked her what the fight was about, and she couldn't even remember.

It seemed to me and to her that it was a terrible shame they didn't speak. One of the most precious relationships they would ever share was effectively allowed to dissolve because of an argument so petty she couldn't even recall its origin.

We all have a 'story' that we tell ourselves and other people about why we are as we are or why we behave in a certain way. It is often an elaborate justification or excuse that we already know in our hearts is not quite true or accurate. Often, especially as we grow older, we get so caught up in the story and so busy holding on to it that it prevents us from moving into a new future.

Nothing in life really has any meaning other than the meaning we ascribe to it. I don't know what happened to those sisters, but if I was a gambling man I'd bet it was based on a simple misunderstanding and each sister played a part in that mix-up that effectively destroyed their relationship. Neither, probably because of pride or ego, sought to clear up the misunderstanding, and they certainly didn't choose to laugh it off and move on together. But they could have.

To paraphrase Richard Bandler, co-founder of the neuro-linguistic programming (NLP) model, if at some point you are going to look back and laugh, why wait? Start laughing now and move on.

If you want to effectively bounce into a new and better future regardless of what you face, you absolutely must forget the past and press forward. Remember what Viktor Frankl said when he realised that the guards were going to destroy his precious manuscript: 'At that moment I saw the plain truth and did what marked the culminating point of the first phase of my psychological reaction: I struck out my whole former life.' He struck out his whole former life. What a powerful, courageous choice!

How can we see the opportunities that are all around us every day if we are busy looking in the wrong direction? It's like carrying around a heavy backpack — you need to put it down and move forward unhindered.

Nelson Mandela is a man who knows a thing or two about forgetting the past and pressing forward. In his autobiography, *Long Walk to Freedom*, he recalls he was just nine years old when his father died of tuberculosis; it was a terrible blow to the young boy, who defined himself by his father. He talks of having to pack up all he'd ever owned and leave the only place he'd ever known to press forward into a new life.

It's well known that Mandela served 27 years in prison for his role as leader of Umkhonto we Sizwe, the armed wing of the African National Congress (ANC). Eighteen of those 27 years were spent in a tiny cell on Robben Island, where he was subjected to sustained cruelty from the white Afrikaner guards and endured hard labour. Apartheid has gone down as a stain on the historical record of South Africa and it would have been easy for Mandela to change into an angry and bitter man, but he didn't. Instead he used adversity to forge the character that would make him one of the most revered and loved leaders of all time. Mandela believed that if he could get through to his guards, 'the most unrepentant racists in the world', then surely he could reach the rest of the world with his message of peace and reconciliation. By using his intelligence, charm, integrity and dignified but resolute defiance he won over even the most brutal prison guards. He was finally released from Pollsmoor Prison in February 1990.

In an effort to prevent the violence that threatened to erupt following ANC leader Chris Hani's assassination in 1993, Mandela addressed the nation to appeal for calm:

> I am reaching out to every single South African, black and white, from the very depths of my being. A white man, full of prejudice and hate, came to our country and committed a deed so foul that our whole nation now teeters on the brink of disaster. A white woman, of Afrikaner origin, risked her life so that we may know, and bring to justice, this assassin . . . Now is the time for all South Africans to stand together against those who . . . wish to destroy what Chris Hani gave his life for — the freedom of all of us.

In 1994, a year after Hani's death, Nelson Mandela became the first democratically elected president of South Africa. He was 74 and held the position until stepping down in 1999.

Mandela has been honoured by more than 250 awards internationally including the 1993 Nobel Peace Prize. He could have exploited his story of injustice — it was a powerful story. He could have dwelled on his 27 years behind bars to become embittered and hell-bent on revenge, but he chose a different future and changed the world as a result.

**NEVER LOOK BACK UNLESS YOU ARE PLANNING TO GO THAT WAY.**

**– HENRY DAVID THOREAU**

Learn from your past so you don't keep repeating the same mistakes. Often your past can help to put your life in context, but once you've done that, let it go. Get real about your current situation and forge ahead to something better.

I once heard Gerry Harvey, CEO of furniture retailer Harvey Norman, speak about waiting for the good old days to return. He suggested that all businesses run in cycles; businesspeople just need to hang on and the good times will return and they can bounce back. The implication is that bouncing back only requires time so that the status quo can return. It's certainly a lot easier to go back to the way things were because we are familiar with that — we know what it feels like and what to expect.

Social psychologist Robert Cialdini has identified one of the strongest forces of influence as 'consistency'. In other words, we are instinctively drawn back to what we know; we like the idea of bouncing back because the past is familiar and there is a sense of 'getting back to normal'. This impulse is so strong that even if a situation is terrible its very familiarity often makes it more attractive than an unknown alternative. It is consistency, for example, that keeps people in abusive relationships or in a job they hate. The need to remain consistent also keeps people hanging on to strategic decisions or outdated business practices long after they cease to be productive.

When we work for the return of the good old days we are involved in *reactive* innovation, but what will really transform a business and a life is *proactive* innovation. Table 4.1 illustrates the contrast between the reactive and proactive innovation approaches.

**Table 4.1: reactive versus proactive innovation**

| Innovation through bouncing back | Innovation through bouncing forward |
| --- | --- |
| Strategising to return to how things used to be — irresponsible and will most likely have a negative impact | Strategising by learning from the past but looking forward to create something better — smart business practice |
| Optimistic for sales to return to how they were — optimism is good; doing the same thing and expecting different results is not | Optimistic to create new practices for sales to be better than they were — forward thinking and activating optimism to make it work for you |
| Focusing on previous wins to imitate | Learning from and building on what worked, then growing into something better |
| Waiting for crisis before igniting innovation | Continuous innovating |
| Recapturing customers who have left | Continuous improvement strategies aimed at *never* losing customers |
| Managing crisis through reactive processes | Strategies for crisis management in place and ready |
| Waiting for declines in productivity and profitability before innovating | Always innovating for continuous growth |

| Innovation through bouncing back | Innovation through bouncing forward |
|---|---|
| Staff engagement and collaboration in crisis mode | Staff engagement and collaboration within the business DNA and culture |
| The past = the future | The future is yet to be created |

Sometimes good enough is simply not good enough anymore. There is no return to the good old days, so the only real option is to forge ahead and create something new, to unleash the power of proactive innovation. Bouncing forward is about stepping into creativity and into a future that we've never experienced before. If you have never experienced that future then you must be ready, open, creative and innovative.

## Start bouncing

*What's your story?*

Take a moment to think about the challenge you face right now. What story have you created about this crisis that links back to your past in some way? Have you assumed that this crisis is going to work out like something similar in your past? What story from your past are you allowing to dictate your future?

## 2 EXPECT THE BEST

Moving forward into a new future requires a new mindset and the diligence to maintain that mindset in the face of all obstacles. Expecting the best is a habit you can foster over time.

In 1957 Robert K. Merton coined the term *self-fulfilling prophecy* when he wrote in his book *Social Theory and Social*

*Structure*, 'The self-fulfilling prophecy is, in the beginning, a false definition of the situation evoking a new behaviour which makes the original false conception come true. The specious validity of the self- fulfilling prophecy perpetuates a reign of error. For the prophet will cite the actual course of events as proof that he was right from the very beginning.'

If you get into the habit of expecting the best, then you have a much greater chance of experiencing the best. And the same is true of other people. If you think highly of the people in your team, encourage them and expect the best from them, then more often than not they will rise to meet those expectations. If, however, you start with a 'false definition' and think your people are useless and have to be micro-managed all the time, then you can be pretty confident that those people will fall in to meet those expectations too.

Whatever expectations you have of yourself and others will 'evoke a new behaviour which makes the original false conception come true'. Say you assume your people are fairly inept and that you need to watch them like a hawk. The fun part comes when you then get to point to the resulting incompetence and say, 'I told you so.' Of course it was probably your expectations rather than your people that caused the outcome. If someone expects you to screw up and is ready to find a way to blame you or ridicule you regardless of what you do, then you are not going to be very motivated to deliver above-average performance.

This phenomenon, according to which people will rise or fall to meet their own or other people's expectations, is sometimes called the Pygmalion effect. Its name derives from the play by George Bernard Shaw, which inspired the film *My Fair Lady*, in which a professor makes a wager that he can teach an uneducated flower girl to behave like a lady. The same premise is used in the film *Trading Places*, with Eddie Murphy and Dan Aykroyd.

Harvard social psychologist Dr Robert Rosenthal demonstrated just how influential expectations can be in shaping reality through his now-famous experiment called 'Pygmalion in the Classroom'. At the start of the academic year Rosenthal assessed 18 classes of elementary school students using nonverbal intelligence tests. Twenty per cent of the students were then identified as 'intellectual bloomers'. The bloomers were identified to their teachers, who were told they could expect to see significant intellectual gains from those particular children in the coming year.

Eight months later all the children were retested, and sure enough the children previously labelled as the 'intellectual bloomers' *had* actually increased in IQ points over the rest of the group. Of course none of the teachers were the least bit surprised by this news — that is, until they were told that the 20 percent had in fact been chosen completely randomly and the initial test was part of the ruse.

The only explanation for this result was that the *expectation* of improvement created a 'false definition' in the mind of every teacher, which provoked new behaviour in the teachers, which in turn affected the children. The teachers in Rosenthal's experiment formed expectations of ability and intelligence based on what they had been told. From the outset they pigeonholed each child as smart or average, and this assumption influenced their teaching style and behaviour toward each child, which in turn affected student outcomes. It was a perfect example of a 'self-fulfilling prophecy'.

Imagine for a moment that Jonny was one of the children identified as an 'intellectual bloomer'. Immediately his teacher, Miss Jones, raised her expectations of him, and because she now 'knew' that Jonny was smart she spent more time with him. After all, 'at least he would appreciate that extra effort'. So when Jonny was confused or needed additional support to understand a topic she was happy to provide it, and she was much more encouraging of Jonny because of his potential. On the flip side, if Jonny made a lot of mistakes Miss Jones was much more likely to put it down to a lapse in concentration and to maintain her encouragement. Miss Jones's new expectations of Jonny based on his 'bloomer' label changed her behaviour toward him and massively influenced their day-to-day interactions.

Also in Miss Jones's class was Suzie, who had not been labelled as a bloomer. This was a little surprising to Miss Jones because she had expected Suzie to do well in the test. It was now evident to the teacher that she had been wrong about Suzie so when she is hard pressed to meet all the needs of her students or to give them individual attention, who do you think she's going to focus on? Suzie isn't encouraged and individually supported in the same way Jonny is because, with limited time, Miss Jones feels justified in offering greater support to the students with the highest potential. What's worse is that even if Suzie aces a test or does exceptionally well on her homework, Miss Jones's immediate response is one of suspicion or she will simply put it down to a fluke. If Suzie becomes disruptive as a result of this lack of attention, then it simply confirms that she's going nowhere. Purely as a result of the labels ascribed to these children, Miss Jones has changed her behaviour, and it is this change of behaviour that persuades her of the accuracy of the labels, not the intellectual ability of each child.

The outcome of the experiment was an increase in IQ by the bloomers and no increase for the rest and yet the only difference between the two groups was their teacher's expectation of their potential. The 'specious validity' of the claim that some were more able than others set in motion a 'reign of error'. The 'bright' kids were encouraged and helped to become better, which they did. The average kids were effectively written off because they were not expected to improve, and they didn't.

In another example of the impact of expectation, Dr David Sobel, a placebo specialist at Kaiser Hospital in California, tells the story of a doctor who was treating an asthma patient. This particular patient was having trouble breathing so his doctor ordered a sample of a new drug he thought might alleviate his symptoms. Within moments of receiving the new drug the patient showed a marked improvement. To test if the drug was really as effective as it appeared to be, when the patient had another attack his doctor gave him a placebo instead of the new drug. A placebo is an inert medication such as a sugar pill that is given in place of a drug as a control. The placebo effect, which often produces miraculous improvements in medical symptoms or conditions, is still one of the most puzzling phenomena in modern medicine. In this instance, however, the placebo didn't work and the patient complained that something must be wrong with the prescription because his breathing was still extremely laboured. Naturally the doctor assumed that the new drug must be effective after all. At least he did until he received a letter from the drug company apologising for accidentally sending him a placebo! Unknown to the doctor he had administered a placebo both times. The only explanation for the improvement was the doctor's attitude, expectations and enthusiasm when administering the first drug as opposed to the second, which he expected to fail.

There is no doubt that expectations affect outcomes. In his brilliant book *The Biology of Belief*, Bruce Lipton tells the story of physician Clifton Meador who reported the following case of *nocebo* (that is, a negative outcome based on expectation). One of Meador's patients, Sam Londe, a retired shoe salesman, was diagnosed with cancer of the oesophagus. At the time this type of cancer was considered 100 per cent fatal and although Londe was treated the medical experts involved 'knew' it was futile. So when Londe subsequently died no-one was very surprised — until they conducted the autopsy. Although they did find cancer in his body there was nowhere near enough to kill him. Londe died because he believed he was going to die and he expected to die. Perhaps more importantly, he died because his expert medical team expected him to die.

What we believe is possible matters and what we expect of ourselves and others matters. Expect the best from yourself and others and you may be surprised by the results.

## Start bouncing

### What are your expectations?

Take a moment to think about the last major challenge you faced. What were your expectations of that event? Did you expect the best or did you assume the worst? Take some time to consider other past experiences. Do you get what you expect?

Now, thinking about the current situation, what are your expectations? If they are bleak, take a moment to revise them, substituting a solution that is both inspiring and compelling.

## 3 EMPOWER YOUR STRENGTHS

For too long we have been told that we should find out what our innate strengths and weaknesses are and spend at least some of our time working on our weaknesses. This may sound logical, especially in a business context, but it's also pointless and extremely difficult to do. And that's not just my opinion.

When I had the good fortune of meeting Sir Richard Branson at a speaking event we were both involved in, I asked him what he considered the secret to his success. He suggested that it was that he surrounded himself with people who were strong in his weaknesses. He ensured that within his proximity he had access to all the abilities and strengths that the business needed to forge ahead while also allowing him to amplify his strengths. Proximity is power.

Branson is not alone in his outlook. The book *First, Break All the Rules* by Marcus Buckingham and Curt Coffman is the product of two mammoth research studies undertaken by the Gallup Organization over a 25-year period, which gave voice to over one million employees and 80 000 managers. Buckingham and Coffman found that the greatest managers in the world *seem* to have little in common — they differ by gender, age and race and employ a vast range of management styles. Yet despite their differences, they all agree on the need to empower strengths. According to the data collected by Gallup, people don't change that much, at least not unless *they* want to. In a business context it is therefore not very productive trying to force people to change through education training or bullying. Instead draw out what's already naturally there and empower individuals to use their strengths.

What we are talking about here is talent. Probably more has been written about talent in recent years than just about anything else. For centuries we have been fascinated by the idea, yet it's only been in the past 30 years that scientists have really started to assess talent in any great depth. But according to Geoff Colvin, author of *Talent Is Overrated*, scientists have come up empty. Having looked into top-level performance in a wide range of fields, from management to surgery to creative writing, the overwhelming conclusion is that there is no such thing as natural talent. What separates the very good from the rest is their willingness to invest thousands of hours in practising and honing their skill.

One widely quoted study led by psychologist K. Anders Ericsson at Berlin's elite Academy of Music concluded that there was no such thing as a 'natural'. There wasn't a single student who 'floated effortlessly to the top while practising a fraction of the time their peers did'. Nor were there any 'grinds' — 'people who worked harder than everyone else, yet just didn't have what it takes to break the top ranks'.

The upshot of this and countless other research studies is that talent is the natural consequence of at least 10 000 hours of deliberate consistent practice. Neurologist Daniel Levitin states, 'In study after study, of composers, basketball players, fiction writers, ice skaters, concert pianists, chess players, master criminals, and what have you, this number comes up again and again . . . No- one has yet found a case in which true world-class expertise was accomplished in less time. It seems that it takes the brain this long to assimilate all that it needs to know to achieve true mastery.'

This is the reason why it's so important to empower your strengths and leave your weaknesses to someone else. Talent is not the result of some happy genetic accident; it's the outcome of effort and hard work over the long term, and frankly there is no way that you will be able to force yourself to clock up the necessary hours on a weakness. If it's a weakness you will not enjoy doing it. If you don't derive any pleasure from the activity, then you simply will not be able to turn it into a skill.

When we think of talent we imagine a brilliant violinist or sports star, but talents don't always have to be so glitzy and for most of us they are not. We all have abilities in certain areas that are better than most people's. Your job is to find out what those things are for you and the people in your team and to use those strengths regularly. Using our signature strengths on a daily or regular basis is one of the best ways for us to be happy, creative and productive.

Often, especially in my industry of personal development and motivation, we can get lulled into the idea that we can be anything we want to be if we just try hard enough. In theory the idea has merit and certainly I think we need to believe in ourselves, but the reality is, as always, a little different. First you need to identify your signature strengths and then you need to match your aspirations to those strengths, because unless you are good at something or show ability in a particular area and enjoy that activity, then you simply will not stick with it long enough to achieve mastery.

This idea is crucial to success of any type and it's especially true in helping you and the people around you to bounce forward into a new life. Too often these natural strengths are ignored or squashed by an education system that is only interested in a very narrow definition of intelligence.

One man who is trying to address this is Dr Howard Gardner, Hobbs Professor of Cognition and Education at the Harvard Graduate School of Education. In 1983 Garner developed the theory of multiple intelligences and suggested that measuring intelligence based on IQ was far too limited. The expanded areas of intelligence that Dr Gardner proposed may help you to consider a far wider range of abilities that you and your team already possess. They are:

» verbal-linguistic intelligence (good with words and language)

» logical-mathematical intelligence (good with numbers)

» visual-spatial intelligence (good with visual images)

» bodily-kinaesthetic intelligence (good with physical things/the body)

» musical intelligence (good with musical instruments and sounds)

» interpersonal intelligence (good with people)

» intrapersonal intelligence (good with self-management)

» naturalistic intelligence (good with nature and the environment).

Dr Gardner also believes that most of our signature strengths and innate abilities are completely ignored in modern schooling and that if we learned to recognise and value them properly in ourselves and others, more people would be doing what they loved and were good at. And if more people were using their signature strengths, then businesses and individuals would be happier, more creative and significantly more productive.

## Start bouncing

### Focus on your strengths

Take a moment to consider the unique abilities and attributes that you possess. This is not always as easy as it sounds. Look through the list of eight expanded areas of intelligence identified by Gardner to see if they ring any bells. Also, it's worth remembering that when we have a special skill or ability and therefore find certain tasks straightforward, we usually assume that the task is easy and that everyone can do what we are doing. Ask your family, friends or work colleagues what they consider your strengths to be. Return the favour and help the people around you to identify and own their unique abilities. Make a list of your top five strengths.

Take a moment to consider how best to use those strengths to help navigate your current crisis.

## 4 STAY ALIGNED AND MOTIVATED

Empowering your strengths will also allow you to stay aligned to what's important and meaningful to you. The best way to continuously bounce forward into a better life following a crisis is to use that crisis to re-evaluate your position, reconnect to what's really important to you and use that knowledge to carve out the new path.

Of course it is one thing to align yourself to your own purpose and why, but how do you manage this dynamic in a business? One CEO and business innovator who is constantly coming up with new ways to achieve this is Ricardo Semler. Semler is the 'sometimes CEO' of Brazilian powerhouse Semco. When he initially joined the family business the usual sparks flew between father and son, but in a show of incredible trust, Semler senior transferred his shares to his 21-year-old son and went on holiday, leaving him in charge. By the end of Semler junior's first day in the job he'd sacked 60 per cent of the senior managers. And he's been breaking the rules ever since.

Originally in shipbuilding, Semco has since diversified into manufacturing, professional services and high-tech software. The workforce has grown from a few hundred to more than 3000 employees.

There are many things that make the 'industrial democracy' of Semco different. There is no hierarchy, no job titles and business cards, no job descriptions or organisational charts, no personal assistants and no planning beyond six months. There isn't even a fixed CEO. Employees choose their own salary and are encouraged to put personal satisfaction before corporate objectives. To this end Semler has introduced some remarkable initiatives that recognise that most people are too busy working to pursue their external passions and interests, and when they eventually do have the time they are too old or tired to want to!

His retire-a-little program, for example, allows staff to buy back work days from the company so they can spend more time with their family or pursuing a passion. Then once they do retire they can choose to sell back the days they took off earlier in their career. That way the retiree gets some extra income and the business maintains access to their vast expertise.

According to Semler, part of what makes this unorthodox approach work is the fact that he has an 'added 30 per cent faith in human nature'. Semler believes that if you treat people like adults and not children and encourage them to seek opportunity and challenge inside or outside work, they will always end up making a bigger contribution to the business. And considering that under his ownership Semco's revenue grew from US$4 million to in excess of US$212 million, he just might be right.

The fact is most people want to feel that their contribution matters, that they are trusted and appreciated. When they do their output is vastly improved and when they don't they simply grind out their day waiting to go home and watch TV. What Semler did, whether he was aware of it or not, was allow people to align themselves to their own goals, which in turn tapped into their innate motivation.

In chapter 2 I introduced self-determination theory (SDT), developed by Edward Deci and Richard Ryan to explain the components of motivation. If we can understand why we feel motivated in some situations and unmotivated in others, then we can learn how to manipulate the situation or alter the environment so we feel more motivated more often, which in turn will help us to bounce forward after a crisis.

Deci and Ryan believe that motivation comes from our human need for autonomy, competence and relatedness. When these needs are met we are motivated, happy, creative and productive. When they are not met our positivity and productivity plummet and we are far less likely to find solutions to pressing problems.

## Autonomy

Autonomy relates to our need for some sense of control over what we do. We need to feel we have some control over what we do each day.

Dr Ellen Langer, a professor of psychology at Harvard University, and her colleague Judith Rodin conducted a now-famous study that demonstrates the significance of autonomy and how being mindful of day-to-day activities can lead to a more engaged life. Langer split the residents of a nursing home into two groups. The first group were encouraged to actively seek out ways to make more decisions for themselves. For example, they were allowed to decide when they would see visitors or when to watch movies. Each participant was also encouraged to choose a house plant. They could decide where to put the plant in their room and how often it needed to be watered; it was their responsibility to keep it healthy.

The second group of residents, which became the control group, were not given the same choices. Although they also had a house plant, they did not choose the plant themselves and instead were simply assigned one by their nurse, who then took all responsibility for watering the plant.

After 18 months the residents from the first group were found to be more cheerful, active and alert. Those who were given even marginally more control of their choices were also healthier than the other group. And perhaps most surprisingly, the autonomy afforded the first group also affected their life expectancy. Less than half as many residents from the engaged group died over the term of the experiment compared with the group who could not exert any autonomy in their daily lives.

In order to feel genuinely motivated so we can actively craft a new life following crisis it's important that we feel a sense of autonomy. We need to feel as though what we do matters and that we can exert some meaningful control over what we do, when we do it, how we do it and who we do it with.

And if this is true for you then it is also true for everyone in your team. If you have a business crisis or difficulty, the quickest way to solve it is to involve your people and empower them to help you. Expect the best from them and then give them the space to get on with the job.

## Competence

Mihaly Csikszentmihalyi, another pioneer in positive psychology, introduced the idea of *flow*. If you have ever lost yourself in an activity that you are competent at or enjoy, then you are experiencing flow. It is often used in the context of athletes, artists or writers who become so engaged in the activity they lose track of time. Csikszentmihalyi calls these moments 'autotelic experiences', from the Greek *auto*, meaning 'self', and *telos*, meaning 'goal' or 'purpose'. When someone experiences flow the task or activity is the reward, because they are able to demonstrate a feeling of competence. The reward is the movement toward mastery. Experiences of flow are not just immensely satisfying; they create positivity and are also good for our health.

In a series of revelatory experiments Csikszentmihalyi assessed what sort of experiences created flow in the daily lives of his study participants. Some people experienced it at work doing certain tasks, some while cooking or tinkering with their car, working out at the gym or engaging in a hobby. One woman even loved washing the dishes because it was useful and also allowed her some guilt-free time to fantasise about her life! The activities were as varied as the people in the study.

Once the participants had identified the activities they were then instructed to *stop* doing those activities. The results were almost immediate. People became sluggish, began complaining of headaches and had difficulty concentrating. Csikszentmihalyi noted, 'After just two days of deprivation . . . general deterioration in mood was so advanced that prolonging the experiment would have been unadvisable.' In fact, just 48 hours without the opportunity to demonstrate competence in anything, regardless of how trivial, resulted in symptoms that were remarkably similar to serious psychological disorder.

In a work setting you can usually reward or punish people into compliance, but you will never activate intrinsic motivation without allowing your people to feel competence. You will never activate innovation, creativity and positivity unless you create a working environment that fosters flow instead of shutting it down.

It's easy to read about these things and dismiss them as psychobabble or New Age nonsense, but understanding human behaviour is the fastest way to initiate a corporate turnaround. Csikszentmihalyi met with Nobel Prize winning economists Gary Becker, George Stigler and Milton Friedman, who considered motivation and the understanding of human behaviour to be the most important issue in modern economics. Much to Csikszentmihalyi's 'incredulous surprise', each believed that modern economics failed to adequately account for human behaviour in a business setting.

### Relatedness

Relatedness involves our need to connect with other people and goes back to the principle of Proximity is Power (chapter 2). When connected to others we like, respect or care about, we are capable of far more than we could ever do on our own.

Nothing of merit can be achieved alone. Besides, success of any sort without others to share it with is always going to be a fairly hollow experience. We are in many ways defined by the people in our lives and the connections and relationships we have. Family, friends, work colleagues, even the people we don't like, influence us, even if only as a warning about what *not* to be.

Whether you are experiencing a business crisis or your crisis is closer to home, actively creating an environment in which you and the people around you can feel autonomous, competent and related will help to activate the third motivational drive that Harlow hinted at back in the 1940s. Fear and greed, carrot and stick motivation, and divide and conquer management are not working, and it's only going to get worse. We need to adapt.

Behavioural scientists often divide tasks into 'algorithmic' and 'heuristic'. Algorithmic tasks are routine, often repetitive tasks that follow a set path to a particular outcome. Algorithmic tasks were very popular during the Industrial Revolution. The father of modern economics and capitalism, Adam Smith, encouraged business toward the division of labour, which meant that most people in the workforce performed one specific, routine algorithmic task. If you want to motivate people to do algorithmic tasks, which are often rote, monotonous and boring, then reward and punishment *will* work.

Heuristic tasks, however, are very different because the outcome doesn't follow a set path and can be reached in a number of different ways. Someone engaged in heuristic tasks will need to experiment for best results and may have to come up with something new. If you want to motivate people to do heuristic tasks that involve using personal experience and common sense, then reward and punishment will *not* work.

A hundred years ago the average employee spent most of his or her time on algorithmic tasks, but according to McKinsey & Company, algorithmic, task-based jobs will account for only 30 percent of job growth now and into the future. This means that heuristic work will account for 70 per cent of job growth. And because heuristic work does *not* respond to reward and punishment we need to get much smarter in how we engage the people in our work teams to elicit their own intrinsic motivation generated by autonomy, competence and relatedness.

When we feel we exert some control over our lives, when we have the opportunity to demonstrate competence and ability so we can feel useful and valued, and when we can engage with others, we are happy, motivated and creative. When we and the people around us are individually and collectively positive and motivated, no crisis seems insurmountable. Nothing is impossible!

I was lucky because my accident brought my purpose very clearly into focus. My life now is fully aligned to the questions I asked myself when I was in the wrecked car: Am I passionate? Am I caring? Am I making a difference? Everything I do I run past those questions, and I use them to guide my actions and behaviours every day. Because I am aligned to my purpose and know my why, it is easy to stay motivated and to continually bounce into a better and better future. Today my focus is very firmly on creating the *Bounce Movement*, and I'll share more on that at the end of the book. I am constantly excited about what lies ahead. I'm as busy as I was before but it doesn't feel like work anymore. I still have the autonomy I thrive on, I get to experience competence through my speaking engagements and working with individuals and businesses to help them through their personal or corporate turnaround, and I have a wonderful network of people to whom I am deeply related. I am truly blessed.

**SUCCESS IS NOT FINAL, FAILURE IS NOT FATAL: IT IS THE COURAGE TO CONTINUE THAT COUNTS.**
**— WINSTON CHURCHILL**

## Start bouncing

### *Activate self-determination theory*

Moving forward into a new future, take a moment to think about how you can encourage more autonomy, competence and relatedness in your workplace. Don't try to go from zero to hero overnight. If you are a bit of a control freak, for example, start by delegating small tasks and encourage and celebrate the little wins. Don't get caught up in telling people 'how' they need to do a task; instead focus on what the outcome needs to be and allow them the freedom to work out the how for themselves. This will develop autonomy and competence. And accept that they may not do it 'your way' or perfectly according to your standard, but that's okay as long as it's done.

# How to ensure that you bounce forward not back

Learning how to bounce forward is not just something that is applicable to a crisis. It's a permanent mindset that you can foster so you are continually bouncing forward in good times and in bad. Nothing stays the same for long. We are meant to evolve and grow; otherwise we stagnate and die.

In my own life there have been countless times when I've had to bounce forward and not back. Both personally and professionally, through each major moment I've needed to stop looking at going back to where I've been in order to bounce forward into what I can become.

There are three secret ingredients in the bounce forward recipe:

» *Grit:* Grit is such a great word — one that really embodies its meaning. Grit is what you need to focus your attention on the immediate tasks, regardless of how difficult they may be. Grit is what is needed when you need to push through broken systems with limited resources. And grit is what will ignite creative problem-solving initiatives, because your refusal to give up will give you access to new thinking and novel solutions.

» *Courage:* They say courage is not the absence of fear but rather the acceptance of fear and the willingness to do what needs to be done anyway. Having an unstoppable psychology means you will consistently take massive action in the face of adversity and fear.

» *Commitment:* Commitment is necessary for the achievement of any goal, in good times and in bad. Nothing of worth can be achieved without it. Stay focused on the long term, and maintain your vision with positivity and optimism no matter what the circumstances.

You may not have heard of Mary and Doug Perkins, but they showed grit, courage and commitment to create a business that you probably will be familiar with — Specsavers. What made the Perkinses so special was that they were not interested in what used to be. Instead they used another economic downturn, this time in the mid 1980s, to start a business that would turn their industry on its head.

Today Specsavers trades in over 10 countries including the UK and Australia, enjoying an annual turnover in excess of £1.2 billion. Before Mary and Doug came along, buying glasses was a pretty uninspiring activity. It was expensive and there was very limited choice in terms of frames. Mary wasn't interested in the status quo; she had no interest in creating another uninspiring option for jaded customers. She wanted to do something that had never been done before and bounce into a new future of colour, design and choice for the customer at a fair price. The fact that you can now go to one of a dozen eye specialists around the world and buy affordable and attractive glasses was made possible by Mary Perkins's ability to bounce into a future that didn't previously exist!

## The big picture: See your new future

Bouncing forward largely depends on your mindset and whether you are willing to shrug off the past and consciously create a new future. It requires a measure of courage and a healthy dash of commitment, but the benefits far outweigh the risks. And of course you need to believe — in yourself *and* in the idea that something better exists for you in your future. Nothing lasts forever — neither the good times nor the bad — but when you expect to find something better around the corner, then anything is possible.

Our minds are astonishing, and although our understanding has improved over the past few decades we still don't really know what's happening in the six inches between our ears. We do know, however, that it's the most important real estate we'll ever own.

In a now-famous study, four groups of world-class athletes of similar ability were put through their paces in a rigorous training regime that differed slightly for each group:

» *Group I:* 100 per cent physical training

» *Group II:* 75 per cent physical training and 25 per cent mental training

» *Group III:* 50 per cent physical training and 50 per cent mental training

» *Group IV:* 25 per cent physical training and 75 per cent mental training.

When the four groups were assessed prior to their departure for the 1980 Winter Olympics in Lake Placid, Group IV showed the greatest improvement followed by Group III, Group II and finally Group I. Evidently the act of visualising their own improvement and seeing their own future created greater actual improvement than physical training alone!

In his book *Peak Performance,* former NASA researcher and peak performance guru Charles Garfield describes this study and also his own experience of the mind's ability to improve performance. While in Milan three years after the Russians had blitzed the Montreal Olympics with 125 medals including 49 gold, Garfield met Soviet sports psychologists and physiologists. They explained how they incorporated visualisation techniques to improve athletes' performance and how they believed it was the mind rather than the body that held the key to peak performance. And they offered to provide a demonstration.

Hooking Garfield up to a portable EEG machine to measure his brainwaves, an ECG to measure his cardiac activity and an EMG to measure his muscular activity, they interviewed him on his fitness levels and monitored his body. He explained that he hadn't been seriously fit for eight years and during that time he had *once* bench pressed 365 pounds. In recent times he hadn't managed over 280 pounds. Garfield was then taken through a relaxation process and was asked to visualise bench pressing 365 pounds again. He was asked to see his own future and to step into that future in his imagination.

After 40 minutes of guided imagery and relaxation, Garfield recalled, 'The imagery now imprinted in my mind began to guide my physical movements. Slowly and patiently, their voices sure yet gentle, the Soviets led me through the lift. I became convinced I could do it. The world around me seemed to fade, giving way to self-confidence, belief in myself, and then to deliberate action. I lifted the weight! I was absolutely astounded.'

There is no question that we have hidden reserves of potential. In his book *Flow: The Psychology of Happiness: The Classic Work on How to Achieve Happiness*, Hungarian psychologist Mihaly Csikszentmihalyi reminds us:

> Contrary to what we usually believe, the best moments in our lives are not the passive, receptive, relaxing times — although such experiences can also be enjoyable, if we have worked hard to attain them. The best moments usually occur when a person's body or mind is stretched to its limits in a voluntary effort to accomplish something difficult and worthwhile. Optimal experience is thus something that we make happen.

Whether we are trying to build a business or learn a musical instrument, the challenges of that objective provide the opportunities for growth. The failures, setbacks and difficulties are not often pleasant at the time. Yet, Csikszentmihalyi suggests, those moments are often the best moments in our lives:

> Getting control of life is never easy, and sometimes it can be definitely painful. But in the long run optimal experience adds up to a sense of mastery — or perhaps better, a sense of participation in determining the content of life — that comes as close to what is usually meant by happiness as anything else we can conceivably imagine.

Difficulty is a natural part of every life. How you choose to approach it and how committed you are to turning adversity into opportunity, will effectively determine not only your success but also your happiness, confidence and self-esteem.

# Part II
# **The 12-day challenge**

# CHAPTER 5
# The 12-day crisis turnaround challenge

Crisis is inevitable. No-one is immune. None of us can realistically expect to travel through life without experiencing at least one major crisis, whether personal, professional, financial, emotional or spiritual. During these difficult times we are called on to make a choice. Do we crumble under the stress and become less than we were, or do we answer to the rallying call, embrace our unique kairos moment and use the opportunities to reinvent ourselves into someone who is better, stronger and more resilient than before?

It doesn't matter if the crisis we face is our fault or is caused by circumstances beyond our control. The only thing that *really* matters is how we choose to handle it. And that most definitely is within our control.

Throughout each of the four principles of the Bounce theory I have deliberately included exercises and thought experiments, which I hope you have participated in. They are designed to prise open your thinking so you start to shift your perspective and open up to new ideas and possibilities. I hope they have offered you some interesting and useful insights along the way. I have also included simple processes to help you engage the power of each of the principles. Now it's time to bring it all together and apply it to the crisis you are now facing.

The hardest point in any crisis is the moment of impact and realisation. In my case, the crisis began with the physical impact during the car accident but you don't need to be in an accident to feel the impact of a crisis. Whatever it is, wherever it is, there will be a physical, emotional or cognitive collision with the truth. In that moment you will realise there is no going back. Something has changed forever and you are going to need to muster all your resources to change with it. This can be an extremely painful and upsetting moment and downturn is likely, but you need to use the energy of the situation to break through hopelessness and inertia so you achieve bounce as soon as possible.

Often when we face difficult times we mentally 'check out' and our body and mind switch to automatic pilot. We can look like we are functioning but we are not functioning at all. It is crucial that we appreciate this and take back the controls as quickly as possible. Crisis can jumble your thinking and create internal as well as external chaos, and the best way to navigate that chaos and get back into the driver's seat is to have a planned strategy to bounce.

This *12-day crisis turnaround challenge* is that plan. You don't need to make the days consecutive but you do need to commit to the 12 days. Each day, do what is asked of you and engage with the process discussed and you will begin to feel more and more in control. By the end of the 12 days you will be back in charge and ready to do what needs to be done.

## Day 1: Create space — de-clutter your life

In Principle 1 we talked about how crisis creates opportunity. The biological imperative ensures that when in crisis our physiology will rally to the imminent threat and do whatever it takes to survive. Faced with a frustration, a difficult issue or a burden we tend to procrastinate. Instead of tackling it head on we ignore or avoid it. If, however, that frustration or issue escalates into a crisis we take action straight away, because we suddenly appreciate the need to do something about it so as to change the situation.

What then happens is we move into action, but often that effort is wasted energy. It's difficult to see clearly — we can't see the wood for the trees. We know we must take action but the noise and the stress of everything around us can be overwhelming, sometimes blinding us to the best course of action. This is why de-cluttering is such a useful, powerful and yet simple first step.

But before moving into action, take a step back and give yourself some breathing space. The best way to do that is to literally clear space from within your current situation. Nature abhors a vacuum; if you create a vacuum then new air rushes in to fill the void. In the same way, if you create space in your life by clearing out the clutter, new ideas and fresh insights will rush in to fill the space.

One of the first jobs I had while still at school was at a pizzeria. First I was a kitchen hand and then I became duty manager. It was hard physical work, particularly during peak time. Friday nights were the worst, with everyone staying in with a movie and a pizza! I regularly found myself falling behind in my efforts to take all the telephone orders, clean the dishes, make the pizzas and get them out in time. This was in the day when this pizza chain's unique selling proposition was that your pizza would be delivered to your door within 30 minutes or it was free. It was a great marketing tool that helped transform the company from a regional pizza joint to a global phenomenon, but it was a nightmare for those who worked there! The clutter in the kitchen and around the phone prevented us from operating efficiently and we found ourselves losing money, as the pizzas were not getting delivered on time.

So what we did, particularly in the peak times, was de-clutter everything. We even put on another staff member whose job was to focus on consistently cleaning up the mess and clutter to make the kitchen operate more efficiently. This simple step changed everything. It boosted our time effectiveness and we did not give away one pizza for six months straight — a new store record!

If your crisis is personal then day 1 could be about de-cluttering your home. Over the course of a life we can accumulate mountains of stuff that often keeps us locked into our particular story. We'll have clothes that we haven't been able to wear for decades but that remind us of a certain time or event. But sometimes all that stuff can become oppressive and negative. Liberate yourself from your clutter. If you have not worn an item of clothing for more than a year, donate it to charity. Have a major purge of stuff and you might be amazed at how invigorated you feel and how much more open you are to dealing with other situations that are weighing you down.

If your crisis or difficulties are work related then do the same at work. I used to have so much clutter on my desk. I'd come into the office and immediately feel as though I was behind the eight ball, rushing just to catch up. Then I read about this clearing space idea and got rid of all my clutter and it was so liberating. I felt able to breathe again and the sense of space gave me new ideas and inspiration.

## SUMMARY

> » Find the clutter.
> » Clear it out and create space to think.
> » Keep the clutter out.

## Day 2: Get real about the situation

Take a moment to fully engage with your current challenge or problem. If you are in full-on crisis mode, then this will not be difficult as you probably can't think about anything else. Make a note of the key issues. Don't exaggerate the situation and don't ignore it. Writing it down on paper can help you to clarify each issue, organise your thoughts and face the reality of the situation.

Say, for example, your business is suffering from an economic downturn. The tendency is to go to extremes. If you are a natural pessimist you will assume the sky is falling and panic will set in. If you are an optimist you may just stick your head in the sand and assume 'everything will work out'. Neither response is terribly helpful. Getting real about the situation might include assessing exactly what is happening with sales in your business. Do you *know* how bad things are or are you guessing?

In my own situation it was pretty obvious what the crisis was. Once I had woken from the coma and the strongest of the pain medication had worn off I could see with my own eyes that my body was very different. But not all crises are as obvious or transparent. A huge part of the anxiety that we all face in times of crisis is the uncertainty around what's actually wrong, what it means and what to do about it. The reason blame, recrimination or pretending there is no crisis doesn't make you feel any better is because you have done nothing to alleviate the uncertainty. It's not the crisis per se that is necessarily the most upsetting part; it's the 'not knowing' around what is wrong and how to fix it.

You may have witnessed this in the past — for example, when someone you care about was waiting for medical results or when you were waiting to find out if someone you love had arrived safely at their destination. More often the worst part of that process is the uncertainty, not knowing what is actually happening. Even when people find out that they have a serious illness they will often be relieved just to know what is wrong. Many report that even bad news is preferable to uncertainty, because at least now they know what they are up against and can decide on a course of action.

Most of us, whether or not we are naturally optimistic, will fill in the gaps in our knowledge with negativity, worry, and images of doom and gloom. Our biology is wired that way as a survival mechanism, but we need to circumvent that process as quickly as possible. We may be tempted to pretend that the crisis isn't happening or that if we ignore it, it will go away. It won't. Day 2 is all about alleviating the uncertainty and getting real about the situation so we can get to grips with exactly what we are dealing with.

## SUMMARY

- » Don't go to extremes — be realistic.
- » Search for the *real* cause.
- » Breathe and relax then begin to take ACTION.

# Day 3: Gather as much information as possible

The more uncertainty you can eliminate, the better you will feel about the difficulties you are facing. To facilitate that process spend some time on the third day of the 12-day challenge noting everything you currently know about the situation. Write everything down but distinguish between what you know to be true and what you think to be true.

Make a note of all the facts you currently know for sure and what you don't know. Record assumptions, rumours and as many contributing factors as you can. Build up a blueprint of the crisis.

Just dumping everything out of your head onto paper can be hugely cathartic in a crisis. It helps to organise your thinking and removes some of the fear so you don't feel so overwhelmed.

If your sales are down then find out exactly how much they are down from the same time last year. Get a breakdown by region, area and sales personnel. That way you can start to drill down into the sales data to ascertain if sales are really down across the board. Or perhaps you will discover that sales are down for only one or two salespeople or the drop is being felt in only one area. Seek to establish answers for the drop in sales. Has there been a change in legislation that is affecting one region and not others? Has something happened to the salespeople whose performance is dropping? Have you lost any major accounts? If so why?

A really useful technique here is called the 'Three Whys'. Ricardo Semler, CEO of Brazilian powerhouse Semco, talks about this technique in his book *The Seven-Day Weekend*. Semco believes that you should always 'ask why and always ask it three times'. Children do this naturally and drive their parents insane, but it's a great way to get to the truth and learn new information very quickly. It also helps to crystallise thinking and shine a light on assumptions and guesswork so you can quickly draw out the truth. When seeking facts and explanations about why the crisis has happened, push past the first responses and the pat 'it's the economy' answers to drill down into more constructive answers that can help to shape your solution. Ask why at least three times to get to the source of the situation.

Once you have exhausted all the issues and written down everything you can about the crisis, go back through the list to

'PROVE' your statements. Use this acronym to distinguish fact from fiction using the following codes:

**P** = Personal prejudice

**R** = Rumour

**O** = Outdated guess or assumption

**V** = Verifiable fact

**E** = Extra data needed/unknown.

If you feel that your business is suffering because of a weak economy you may end up with a list similar to the following:

1. Sales are down 17 percent on the same time last year. (V)

2. John and Susan's sales figures are responsible for 80 percent of the drop. (V)

3. John has just got married and is expecting a child, which is why his performance has dropped. (V/O/E)

4. Susan is thinking of leaving anyway. (R)

5. Women are not good in sales, especially when things get difficult, because they are less resilient. (P)

6. Product returns have increased by 10 percent on last year. (V)

7. Quality dropped following our switch in supplier. (V/O/E)

8. We need to secure a new supplier. (E)

9. The industry is contracting and the economy is bad. (V/E)

This process allows you to consciously assess all the information you currently have about the situation. It is easy enough to verify if sales are down; it's also easy to see which of the sales team are responsible for the decline in sales. It may be true that John has recently married and is preparing to become a father, but it is unfair to assume that is the reason for his drop in performance. Clearly, extra data is required to establish what is really going on. As for Susan, until you have a conversation with her all you really know is that her performance has dropped. It's unfair and probably inaccurate to base your conclusions on assumptions and prejudices that you hold about Susan or about a woman's ability to work in sales. You can quantify the number of product returns, but you don't know what is causing them. It may be that quality dropped when you first switched suppliers, but a transition period almost always creates teething problems. Until you dig deeper you are basing your knowledge on outdated assumptions when what you really need is verifiable facts. Perhaps a competitor has brought out a better product or offers a better warranty. Hastily adopting solutions that involve considerable time and money, such as finding a new supplier, is short-sighted and probably unnecessary. And if it's not really the issue, then it won't solve the problem so you will have wasted resources fixing the wrong problem.

In a difficult business climate the easy answer is that 'the industry is contracting' or 'the economy is bad'. It's that first pat answer that most business leaders use to justify a dip in results. And it may be true, but thousands of businesses thrive in a downturn so it's not a blanket excuse and it's not even always true. Some sectors will always thrive in difficult economic times. So you need extra data to ascertain whether these explanations are supported by the facts or simply wishful thinking — a convenient excuse for poor performance.

Your job on Day 3 is to keep asking questions so you can establish what is fact and what is fiction or speculation. Once you have removed as much uncertainty as possible you will start to feel more in control and optimistic.

In my own situation, had I created a list it would probably have looked like this:

1. I've lost my right arm. (V)

2. I'll never be able to play guitar again. (O/E)

3. I'm right-handed so I'll have to relearn how to use my left arm, and that's going to take time. (V)

4. I'm going to be a burden to my family because I'm going to be in a wheelchair for the rest of my life. (P/O)

5. I'll be in constant pain. (E)

6. My wife and family still love me. (V/E)

7. I'm not dead. (V)

8. People recover from terrible injuries and go on to live long and successful lives. (V)

It was true that I had lost my right arm. It wasn't as though I could pretend I hadn't. I still felt it and could imagine myself wiggling my fingers, but when I opened my eyes I still only had a stump below my right shoulder. But I also realised that I couldn't pretend to know what was possible. I had no idea if anyone had ever been in this situation before and taught themselves to play guitar again, so I needed extra information on this. When I initially researched the topic and couldn't find anyone who had successfully done so, I just figured I'd be the exception.

I was right-handed so it was going to be a slow road to recovery as I'd need to learn to do with my left hand all the things I used to do with my dominant hand. But it could have been so much worse. I could have lost both! I realised that my personal prejudices were driving the idea that I would be a burden to my family. I had a conservative 'old school' upbringing where the father was the breadwinner and the wife was the homemaker. It didn't occur to me that this was not set in stone or that my key value to my family was something other than my ability to provide for them. As for the pain, I really didn't know and only time would tell. I knew Kate still loved me, but I was nervous when I saw the girls for the first time. I needn't have been. As a reminder of the negative influence of uncertainty, the worry I experienced about what they might think immediately dissolved when they didn't even seem to really notice my disability. And finally, I knew that people recover from terrible injuries all the time.

Part of my recovery process was deliberately researching stories of resilience and survival so I could build up my own database of remarkable people who have survived terrible injuries.

One story that particularly stood out in that research, perhaps also because of the nature of his injury, is Aron Ralston's. In April 2003 Ralston set off for an afternoon canyoneering in Utah's Blue John Canyon. As the name suggests, canyoneering is like mountaineering but in canyons. While not as dangerous as mountaineering there are still safety guidelines, and Ralston broke them all! He didn't tell anyone that he was going to Blue John and he didn't take his mobile phone — two decisions that almost cost him his life. During his descent of a canyon Ralston managed to dislodge an 800-pound boulder that crushed his right arm, pinning him against the canyon wall. Unable to free himself he remained there for five days, hoping someone would discover him. No-one did. He knew he would die unless he took radical action. In an act that demonstrated the extraordinary strength of the human spirit and our innate drive to survive, Ralston broke his own arm, using the boulder to snap his radius and ulna. Then he proceeded to cut his arm off with a blunt penknife. In fact, the knife had been a free gift with a torch he had recently bought, although he never revealed the brand! Having freed himself he then climbed out of the canyon, at one point abseiling down a 20-metre wall. Luckily he was found by a holidaying Dutch family and airlifted to hospital. Ralston's inspirational story was turned into the film *127 Hours*.

Facing his crisis he was forced to get very real about the situation and as his options diminished he was faced with an appallingly difficult choice. In an interview with *National Geographic* he was asked about that decision and answered:

> After having enough sleep-deprived, meandering thoughts about how I arrived in the canyon, I realized that my situation was the result of decisions that I had made. I chose to go out there by myself. I chose to not tell anyone where I was going. I chose not to go with two climbers I had met in the canyon. But I also realized that I had made all of the choices up to that point that had helped me survive. I took responsibility for all of my decisions, which helped me take on the responsibility of getting myself out.

Terrible things happen to good people all the time. When your time comes you must take responsibility, and part of that process is gathering all the information you can about the situation.

## SUMMARY

» Be a detective and search for truth.

» Take responsibility and ownership.

» Write it down and PROVE it.

# Day 4: Determine control

Everything in life, whether professional or personal, can be divided into just two things: the stuff we can control and the stuff we can't control. The vast majority of what we stress about falls into the domain of things we can't control, so all the effort and worry used up around those issues is a pointless waste. Times of crisis or difficulty are hard enough without adding to the pressure by worrying about things we can't influence.

Go back to the list you created earlier and add one of two additional codes:

**C** = Control (i.e. I can control this)

**NC** = No control (i.e. I don't control this).

This step helps you to draw this important distinction so you can immediately reduce your task list and turn down the pressure. I knew, for example, that I couldn't control the fact that I'd lost my arm. I couldn't turn back the clock, so it was pointless lamenting what was. I needed to focus on what was going to be. I knew that whether I played guitar again and how fast I could relearn how to use my left hand were under my control and ultimately came down to my perseverance and commitment. I couldn't really control how much pain I was going to be in, but I could learn to manage it. Releasing the stuff you can't control has an immediate impact on your ability to bounce forward and find opportunity in crisis. The past is the past — let it go.

From a business perspective, there is little you alone can do about the economy. So stop worrying about it, and stop leaning on it. Shrink your focus down to what you can control and you'll immediately feel better.

There is a great story about a man with a hot dog stand. He's got *the* best hot dogs in the city; people go out of their way to buy his hot dogs. He uses the best rolls and the best meat and has a fantastic array of condiments, which turn a great dog into a culinary delight. He's created a very successful business — so successful, in fact, that he decides to set up other hot dog stands. His son, however, is a business graduate and chastises him for being so stupid:

'What are you thinking, Dad? Don't you read the papers or watch the news — the economy is weak and the picture is bleak for years to come. You can't expand.'

His father listens, wide-eyed, to his clever son. 'Oh, I didn't realise. But my business is doing really well.'

'Well, you've been lucky, Dad, but all that's going to change. What you really need to do is contract. You need to cut your costs and batten down the hatches until the economy improves.'

So of course the father, who doesn't have a business degree, decides his son must be right. So he buys cheaper rolls, cuts back on his condiments and decides against buying the freshest and best hot dogs, and he stops advertising in the local paper. Sure enough, trade starts to dry up. Over dinner one night he congratulates his son: 'I can't believe I was going to expand! You really saved me there, son.'

Of course he did not lose business because of the economy; he lost business because he stopped doing the things that made him successful in the first place. He allowed fear rather than fact to dictate his strategy. When the economy shifts down a gear, whether into a recession or just a downturn, people panic. As a result, they stop doing what made them successful and contract — and their industry ends up looking like Swiss cheese, with holes and missed opportunities everywhere. The smart exploit that fear and press on with their strategy. The moral of the story is that if you want to become more efficient and cut back on non-essential spending, then do so, but never change a winning formula just because the media and the nay-sayers tell you that disaster is on the horizon.

In 1982 some nut with a grudge contaminated one of America's most trusted headache tablets with cyanide and several people died. It was a crisis of epic proportions for Tylenol manufacturer Johnson & Johnson. Unable to locate the source of the attack, the company stuck to what had always made them successful — their brand integrity and trust — and withdrew the entire inventory from stores across America.

A total of 31 million bottles of Tylenol were returned to the company, costing them a whopping $100 million, and their market share plummeted from 37 percent to 7 percent. Some analysts saw it as the beginning of the end for the company, and yet today Johnson & Johnson is stronger than ever. They didn't stick their head in the sand and they didn't point fingers of blame or commission expensive reports to explain how it wasn't their fault. They simply reconnected with their 'why' — creating top- quality products that their customers could trust. They informed themselves about the situation really quickly, separated fact from fiction, worked out what they could control and what they couldn't control, and took decisive action. Johnson & Johnson's CEO at the time, James Burke, personally appeared on TV to keep people informed. Their handling of the situation ensured that Johnson & Johnson didn't just bounce back quickly, they bounced forward, emerging as an honest, ethical and trustworthy company willing to put people before profit.

## SUMMARY

> » Don't worry about stuff you can't control.

> » Don't make excuses.

> » Take ownership of what you can control.

# Day 5: Decide who needs to know what and share information

Regarding the situation you find yourself in, take a moment to decide who needs to be kept in the loop. In business it's not always easy or advisable to tell all the team everything, but not all information is top secret. Work out what you can share and who in your team needs to know what, and tell them. Wherever possible, be as open and honest as you can because it fosters a sense of belonging and a willingness to pull together. Try to make sure you share information with people who can do something about that information. There is no point in stressing people out about something over which they have zero control.

In the example of falling sales you would clearly need to speak to the sales manager to find out what he or she feels is happening, and specifically with the performance of John and Susan. You would also need to speak to the manufacturing manager to ascertain what was happening regarding the returns and what the real situation is with the new supplier. Customer services may also be able to shed some light on the returns increase, because they hear direct from customers when problems arise. Depending on the outcome of these meetings it might then be necessary to speak to John and Susan directly to find out what is happening and how you and the team can support them to improve performance. Also, if you discover that there really is a problem with the supplier, then you will need to talk to them direct and perhaps start researching alternative solutions.

It would also probably be useful to hold a sales meeting with everyone involved and seek solutions and ideas for improvement from the whole team. If your business is experiencing a drop in sales, everyone in the sales team will already know. They are probably already worried about what that is going to mean for them, and their imagination will almost always make the situation worse than it really is, so conveying the real situation will probably help to reduce their stress levels. It will also be a warning to those who are not trying hard enough, because now they know that management is aware of it.

Too often business leaders keep the people working in the business in ignorance of the challenges of the business. In some cases, the information is sensitive. Bad news can massively affect share price, so companies with shareholders do need to be careful. But honest and open interaction between management and staff is almost always preferred because it allows people to feel ownership. You also gain access to their experience and knowledge, which may help to throw up solutions you hadn't thought of. So decide who needs to know and share information.

The same is true in a personal crisis. Chances are your family and friends have already noticed that something is wrong. Put them out of their misery and share the challenge with them — especially those parts they can help you with — so they can understand your concerns and be more supportive.

In my situation, many friends and family members came to visit me in hospital. I often think it was as hard for them as it was for me, especially in the beginning when I was in a coma and there was a huge amount of uncertainty about my condition. No-one was sure, for example, whether or not I had brain damage. Kate had already made the decision to keep the details of my accident from our children. They were too young to understand, and besides we really didn't know what would happen so there was no point worrying them unnecessarily. The same was true for many of our friends and family members — the only people who initially knew how bad it was were Kate, Mum, Dad and my immediate family.

They say a problem shared is a problem halved but that's not always the case. If you share a problem with someone when you still have no idea of its extent, or if you confide in someone who loves you but doesn't have any control or ability to help, then the problem shared can be a problem doubled! You have to be smart, sensible and strategic when looking to share information about the crisis you face. Once you have all the facts and you know what you are up against, then get people involved and leverage other people's talents, but until then your job is to assemble all the facts.

Considering your current difficulty ask yourself, who needs to know and what do they need to know?

## SUMMARY

» Be open and honest.

» Share and collaborate.

» Use intuition decisively.

# Day 6: Identify the gaps

Once you've informed the right people and loaded up the right information, then you are in a position to actively collaborate on the solution. Whatever your current crisis, chances are you already have access to the ideas and resources you need to solve it. But you need to identify the gaps and learn to be vulnerable enough to seek those ideas and resources.

The business leader who has decided who needs to know what and opened discussions about the problems won't get all the answers needed. In the conversations that the sales manager has with John and Susan, he or she needs to push past the throwaway answers and actively seek the truth so something constructive can be done.

Speaking to customer service and the manufacturing department, for example, might reveal that no-one really knows why the returns rate has increased, so there is clearly a gap in knowledge that needs to be filled. Someone needs to analyse the data and get to the bottom of the problem and someone needs to be made accountable for that.

For example, I realised that I didn't actually know if anyone who had lost their right arm had ever learned to play guitar again. Until my accident I had no reason to want to know that information. So I identified a gap in my knowledge. I also wasn't sure about the level of pain I would have to live with — no-one knew. That was only ever going to become clear with time.

As I got back on my feet, literally as well as figuratively, I also had to acknowledge that I just didn't know how to manage money. It took a while to accept it, because it felt silly — I was a grown man, after all. But I was never taught how to manage money, and neither was Kate, so how was I ever going to learn what I needed to do unless I accepted my weakness and found someone who could help me plug the gap? I was confident that if I tapped my existing network of contacts I would find someone who could help or who knew someone who could help.

Social networking sites such as Facebook and LinkedIn for business have enormous potential for enabling us to reach out and gain insight, expertise and information that can help to solve our current crisis. Think of my take on six degrees of separation, discussed in chapter 2.

One of the most powerful resources in any business is the ability to foster mentors — people who are more successful than us in certain areas or who have already been through the challenges we face. Most businesspeople know this and yet few act on it. It is, however, the fastest possible way to find and implement solutions and get us where we want to go. And with the technology that is now at our fingertips we don't even need to meet these mentors face to face. An astounding amount of information is already available online. True, you have to be discerning but there are countless online business communities where you can share and discuss your challenge and find others who can offer solutions. And these forums can be as anonymous as you like.

**MEN NEARLY ALWAYS FOLLOW THE TRACKS MADE BY OTHERS AND PROCEED IN THEIR AFFAIRS BY IMITATION, EVEN THOUGH THEY CANNOT ENTIRELY KEEP TO THE TRACKS OF OTHERS OR EMULATE THE PROWESS OF THEIR MODELS. SO A PRUDENT MAN SHOULD ALWAYS FOLLOW IN THE FOOTSTEPS OF GREAT MEN AND IMITATE THOSE WHO HAVE BEEN OUTSTANDING. IF HIS OWN PROWESS FAILS TO COMPARE WITH THEIRS, AT LEAST IT HAS AN AIR OF GREATNESS ABOUT IT.**

**— NICCOLO MACHIAVELLI**

Considering the key professional or personal challenges you now face, what do you not know? And who might be able to provide that information? Who do you know who could help or might know of someone else who could help?

This can be tricky because often we don't know what we don't know, but you will usually know where there are gaps in your knowledge or expertise. Try to identify the critical gaps and match them to a person or external resource that could help you to bridge that gap.

## SUMMARY

- » Be vulnerable and seek solutions.
- » Acknowledge, accept and ask.
- » Identify knowledge gaps and build bridges.

# Day 7: Seek involvement and buy-in from all involved

Crisis of any type implies change. That's why people so often panic when faced with crisis. They feel vulnerable and, as we've discussed, most adults don't like feeling vulnerable.

In 'How Hardwired Is Human Behavior?', an article published in the *Harvard Business Review* in 1998, Nigel Nicholson argues:

> You can ask people to think outside the box and engage in entrepreneurial endeavours all you want, but don't expect too much. Both are risky behaviors. Indeed, any kind of change is risky when you are comfortable with the status quo. And evolutionary psychologists are not surprised at all, by the fact that, despite the excellent press that change is given, almost everyone resists it — except when they are dissatisfied.

Helping others to understand the situation therefore helps to involve them in the process so they don't actively resist any change required. Someone who isn't sure what's going on is much more likely to resist change and seek to exert even greater control over their environment. That isn't always helpful, and it's why communication and collaboration are so critical to crisis management. If you genuinely involve your people so they understand what needs to be achieved, are invited to offer potential solutions, and can help in designing and implementing those solutions, then you won't need to micromanage them all the time.

In 1960 MIT management professor Douglas McGregor wrote a book called *The Human Side of Enterprise*. In it he suggested that issues we had long considered business problems such as inefficiency and poor productivity were actually people problems disguised to look like business problems. What gave McGregor's insights broad appeal was that he didn't just have a PhD in psychology from Harvard — he also had leadership experience. In the book he introduced *Theory X* and *Theory Y*. Theory X is applied by business leaders who believe people are basically lazy and therefore the only way to successfully motivate a workforce is through reward and punishment (carrot and stick). Theory Y is applied by forward-thinking business leaders who believe that people are not idiots and that if you involve them in the challenges they will come up with innovative and effective solutions to business problems.

Despite evidence that Theory Y creates the best business performance, many businesses today are still operated from a profoundly Theory X perspective. And it's costing them dearly. The comprehensive Q12 employee engagement study conducted by Gallup discovered that 24.7 million US workers were actively disengaged from their work, costing the US economy between $292 billion and $355 billion every year. That's more than the GDP of over 150 countries in 2010 including Hong Kong and Singapore! In 2008 Gallup investigated the same issue in the UK and found that disengaged workers cost the UK economy between £59.4 billion ($86.5 billion) and £64.7 billion ($94.2 billion) every year. McKinsey & Company has reported even worse statistics, suggesting that in some countries as few as 2 to 3 percent of the workforce are actively engaged in the work they do every day. That's a terrible waste of resources, ideas and productivity.

Once you have identified who needs to know what and worked out what information or knowledge you are missing, then you need to involve your team in finding a solution. Even if you are in the middle of a personal crisis, it's fair to say that you are unlikely to solve it alone. You need to open the floor for input.

Consider creating brainstorming groups in your business to flesh out the challenges and come up with solutions. Don't just get the salespeople to brainstorm sales problems. Bring in people from different departments to elicit fresh ideas and perspectives. Involve people from manufacturing or customer service or logistics. Make the sessions fun, provide lunch and make it clear that all contributions are welcome, no matter how off the wall. Remember, you and your team will need to think impossible thoughts so you can find solutions you would never have considered on your own.

By involving the people who will eventually implement those decisions you also radically increase the possibility of those people pushing through the change. Social scientists have found that we are much more likely to implement our own ideas or ideas we have been involved in creating and fine-tuning than ideas we have simply been told to implement.

In an experiment conducted by Harvard professor of psychology Dr Ellen Langer, $1 lottery tickets were sold to office workers. The tickets came in matched pairs: the buyer got one and the other ticket was put in a box. It was from this box that the winning ticket would be drawn and the prize was the total collected money from ticket sales. Of the people who bought tickets, half were allowed to choose their own ticket and the other half were given a ticket by the researcher. Several days before the prize draw was due to take place the ticket recipients were contacted to ask if they would be willing to sell their ticket back to the researcher. Those who had chosen their own ticket put a far greater value on their chosen ticket. On average they wanted to be paid $8 for their $1 ticket. Those who did not choose their own ticket were willing to sell their ticket for an average of $2 a ticket. Ten people who chose their own ticket refused to sell at any price, as opposed to just five from the non-choosing group. Langer attributed these results to the illusion of control.

People like to feel they have at least some control over what happens to them, especially when they are facing a crisis. If you involve your team and encourage them to get involved in the challenges the business faces, then you will dramatically increase their engagement in the tasks and activities you want them to complete. If you don't allow them ownership they will not 'buy in' to the solutions you create by yourself.

According to this quirk in human nature, known as the 'endowment effect', we always ascribe more value and therefore more importance to things we choose ourselves or to things we already own. If people in teams are encouraged to engage with the crisis the business faces, then they are much more likely to offer solutions and choose activities, which they will then follow through on because it was *their* idea in the first place. A good plan created by the team will always be much more effective than a perfect plan created by the leader in isolation.

Regardless of the challenge you face, someone somewhere has solved it before. If you have all the facts and you have actively sought to identify and fill the gaps in your understanding, then it's time to open the floor for help and suggestions. No-one likes to be dictated to, and even the best leader does not have all the answers. So get your team together, explain the situation and seek their advice and feedback. You never know, you might just be presented with a solution you would not have thought of on your own. And the person who makes the suggestion is also much more likely to implement that solution. This approach requires courage and trust in your people. But remember the Pygmalion effect: most people will rise or fall to meet your expectations of them, so expect the best and encourage everyone to seek and implement solutions.

## SUMMARY

> » Help others to understand.

> » Seek involvement from all relevant parties.

> » Collaborate, collaborate, collaborate.

## Day 8: Monitor results and fall forward

Of course taking a stand and making a decision that supports your transition through crisis is just part of the journey. Once you get in motion you need to stay in motion and monitor results so you can adapt and continue to make positive progress. You will make mistakes and take some wrong turns but just pick yourself up, learn from it and move on.

I was pretty angry with myself as I lay on the icy ground after breaking my leg again, but staying angry wasn't going to change it. I'd come so far and I'd proven I could defy the odds once, so I resolved to defy them again. I fell but I fell forward and didn't allow the break to break my spirit. I'm sure if I stayed angry for long enough I could even have worked myself up to a point that I would have engaged a lawyer and sued the hospital for failing to spot that I'd broken it in the first place. But the doctor was doing his best. The number of rods and metal plates that were already in my leg meant it was very difficult to identify the break, and besides what good would have come from it? It wasn't going to get me back on my feet any quicker. Only I could do that.

In business it's easy to get into action without really knowing if the action is the right action. When we face difficulties we tend to want to rush in and fix them. As a result we don't get all the facts, we make assumptions and jump to conclusions without really knowing what is causing the crisis in the first place. Then we come up with a bandaid plan that is delegated to someone who had no part in its creation and wonder why it doesn't work!

For example, it would be easy for the business leader experiencing a drop in sales to fire John and Susan and recruit some new salespeople as a knee-jerk 'solution' to the problem. But that's not necessarily going to work. It may be that there are perfectly legitimate reasons for John and Susan's performance drops. It may be that they have both been top sellers in the past, so firing them because of what might be a temporary slump would be short-sighted and counterproductive, as would sourcing a new supplier without getting to the bottom of what is really causing the returns. Imagine if the business leader had jumped on the 'solution' of finding a new supplier — all the time and effort that would take, the disruption to supply as the teething problems were once again ironed out — only to discover that the return rate remained at 10 percent. What a colossal waste of resources!

Crisis requires strength of character and you may need to delve into resources you didn't know you had, but I promise you they are there. You need a strategy and a plan and you need to get into action sooner rather than later. Sometimes, however, we can be so desperate to do something or to be seen to do something that we just get into action without much thought. Although breaking the inertia and getting into motion quickly can be a blessing, the outcome of those actions must be monitored so the strategy can be fine-tuned. Too often businesses embark on a strategy but don't follow up to see whether it is implemented properly and whether the expected results are being achieved. And if you don't monitor results then how can you possibly know if you are on the right track?

If plan A doesn't work so well then assess the plan, work out why it doesn't work and implement plan A1. Take action and assess the outcome. If it fails, tweak it and try again. The only real failure comes when you give up; everything else is just feedback. Remember Sir James Dyson, who created 5127 prototypes of his cyclone vacuum cleaner before he found a model that worked. Dyson often states in interviews that he believes people give up too soon. When it seems like the world is against you, Dyson suggests, '. . . that's the point when you should push a little harder. I use the analogy of running a race. It seems as though you can't carry on, but if you just get through the pain barrier, you'll see the end and be okay. Often, just around the corner is where the solution will happen.'

So take a moment to consider your current situation. Do you have a plan? What is your plan B? Write down what success will look like for you so you are clear what you are aiming for. Also, make a note of the milestones along the way so you know what 'working' looks like and can alter your plan if you fail to meet the milestones.

## SUMMARY

» Pick yourself up, learn and move on.

» Take measurable action.

» Visualise and write it down.

# Day 9: Have fun

No-one loves crisis, although once you master the bounce cycle you will learn to embrace it and even enjoy it. None of us are immune from difficulty, and frankly if we were life would be pretty dull. So whatever your crisis have some fun as you transition through it!

If your crisis is work related then make sure you inject some laughter into the team. It may be a serious situation but you don't need to be serious all the time. Lighten the mood, have a laugh, share stories and take the time to bond with your team. You don't need to go overboard. Bring in a box of doughnuts as a surprise and a thank you for their hard work. Buy a slab of beer and switch to voicemail once a month and just relax and share stories. Ask your people what good things have happened this week and get them to reconnect to their positivity so they maintain the forward momentum.

Work is so frequently viewed as negative. I often hear people say, 'I have no life — all I do is work.' Laughter is a great way to blur the lines between work and life, so bring fun into your workplace. The bonus is that when you get people to relax, communicate more openly, and share their personal stories and histories, you break down the barriers between people. They see a person, not just a colleague, and this fosters vulnerability, which can also assist communication, collaboration and productivity.

We need only think about the Virgin brand to see just how potent fun can be for the bottom line. Sir Richard Branson is fun. When you see him on TV he almost always has a smile on his face and he's usually in the middle of some wacky PR stunt. I was fortunate enough to share the stage with him at a conference in Melbourne, and he's a guy that looks like he's having fun in life. He's also one of the most successful businesspeople of all time. Even in businesses in which he is no longer actively involved his personality still shines through. Before Virgin Mobile in Australia was sold to Optus, for example, the people in that business were every bit as fun-oriented as Branson. Most business leaders need to report their division's quarterly results, but in Virgin Mobile Australia those reviews were a little different. To celebrate another quarter of taking measured risks and seeking new opportunities, the management team were each allocated a dare — from swimming with sharks to learning trapeze to abseiling or aerobatics. The action was then recorded and shared with the team over a few drinks — and a lot of laughter at the sight of managers scared out of their wits!

The Virgin brand is built on Branson's core philosophy: if you keep your staff happy then your customers will be happy, and if you keep your customers happy then your shareholders will be happy. And clearly it works.

Come up with three ideas you could implement immediately that would not cost much but could bring a smile to the faces of the other people going through this crisis with you. Use the crisis to pull you closer together as a team or business unit and laugh away some of the stresses and strain.

### SUMMARY

» Inject purposeful laughter.

» Relax and communicate.

» Bring a smile with you everywhere.

## Day 10: Focus on the cause not the symptoms

To maintain forward-moving positivity focus on the cause of the challenges, not the symptoms. Going back a few years the music industry focused all its attention on the symptoms and paid a pretty heavy price for it. They were so consumed by the fact that people were using free download sites such as Napster that they focused a full-scale legal assault on the symptom without considering the cause. Yes, people were downloading free music but the music industry did not stop to ask why. They wanted to maintain the lucrative status quo that had existed for decades. Their market, however, was changing — music fans didn't want to buy albums, just songs, and they were moving away from a physical product to digital music downloads that they could play on their iPod or MP3 player. By the time the music industry started to focus on the cause Apple had already stepped in to create iTunes, and the game was changed forever.

If your market is changing then resisting that change is pointless. Look at the point-and-click camera market, for example. That's a tough retail space. Most mobile phones have a camera built in and most smartphones have a better-quality camera than many lower end point-and-click cameras! The challenge the camera companies face is that everyone already carries their phone everywhere with them. They can take a picture and send it to a friend or upload it to Facebook in seconds. Focusing on the cause and not the symptom, camera companies are adapting to add upload features to their cameras so they can compete with smartphones. They are also focusing on areas of photography that the smartphone will never address.

If your sales have fallen as a result of a poor economic environment, is it just the environment? Is it possible that your market is shifting? Could it be that your customer wants something more or something different from the products or services you are currently supplying? Have your competitors come out with something that is capturing the hearts and minds of your customers? If you don't really know then you need to find out. Your customers are getting more discerning. Most can easily compare features and prices using the internet, and they won't suffer poor service or shoddy products. The days of the angry letter or disgruntled email are over. If your customers are unhappy then they are liable to tweet about it, blog about it or even post a video on YouTube.

In 2008 Canadian musician Dave Carroll and his band Sons of Maxwell were due to tour Nebraska for a few weeks. So they booked flights from Halifax, Nova Scotia, to Omaha, Nebraska, with United Airlines, connecting through Chicago's O'Hare Airport. Like most musicians they looked after their guitars with as much care as you would a small child. Most parents, of course, would prefer to take their children with them on board, but United insisted that the guitars be checked into the baggage hold. Reluctantly the band relinquished their beloved instruments. Then while on the tarmac at Chicago waiting to disembark Dave, his mates and some other passengers saw baggage-handling crew throwing guitar cases on the tarmac. As theirs was a connecting flight it wasn't until the following day that Dave discovered that his $3500 Taylor guitar had been broken.

For almost a year Dave tried to get United to compensate him for this loss. They refused and he was passed from pillar to post. Eventually Dave got sick of the run-around and in his last email exchange with United he told them that he was going to write a song about United and post it online.

You can just imagine the apathetic 'customer service' representative receiving this email and probably having a good laugh about the 'threat'. The song 'United Breaks Guitars' was posted on YouTube on 6 July 2009. No-one in United was laughing for very long. Within 24 hours the catchy little song had been viewed by more than 150 000 people; within three days half a million people had seen it. As of writing, the clip has been viewed almost 13 million times. On its own the clip was a public relations nightmare but the media also ran with the story, further damaging the United brand *The Times* (London) reported that the video was responsible for a 10 percent drop in United share price, wiping some $180 million off the value of the stock.

In short, you should know if your customers are happy — and if you don't know, ask them. The good news for Dave and his band is that Bob Taylor, owner of Taylor Guitars, offered him two new ones. And United now uses his video for internal training purposes.

Whatever crisis you face, if you are to leverage positivity for success you need to stay mindful of relevance. There is no point in focusing all your energy on solving a crisis that will just resurface six months down the track because you were so distracted by the symptom that you forgot to address the cause. How relevant will your products and services be in the future? If you don't know, find out. Ask your customers and listen to what they say.

My friend Michael McQueen, an expert on relevance, says, 'Relevance is not just about success, it's about your very survival.' In business we need to constantly evaluate our relevance with our wider audience so we stay one step ahead of client expectations. Constant and never-ending improvements to our products and services will ensure a more successful, productive and profitable future.

If your crisis is more personal in nature, it's still important to focus on the cause and to tackle that rather than spending time masking the symptom.

### TAKE AWAY THE CAUSE, AND THE EFFECT CEASES.
### – MIGUEL DE CERVANTES

Spend a few minutes thinking about what has actually caused the challenges you now face. Forget about what those causes have created and focus on getting back to the source. Once you have highlighted the causes, think about how many you have control over.

In addition, regardless of your crisis situation, take a few minutes to really think about your product and service offerings now. Imagine you have a crystal ball and are able to see the future. Fast forward one, five and ten years in your mind — will your products and services still be relevant? Think about what may change in your market, how your customers may adapt and how their expectations may increase. Are you ready for that or not?

Make a note of the products or services that are most vulnerable and write down three ideas for improving each so you maintain relevance over the long term.

In his book *A Whole New Mind*, Daniel Pink suggests that the business landscape is changing forever because of 'Abundance, Asia and Automation'. We have so much stuff, and access to so much stuff, that everything is getting cheaper, which is also influenced by Asian productivity and automation. He suggests that to stay relevant we all must seek to answer the following three questions:

» Can someone overseas do it cheaper?

» Can a computer do it faster?

» Is what I'm offering in demand in an age of abundance?

If the answer to the first two questions is yes and the answer to the last is no, then clearly you've got problems. Pink suggests that the problems we now face will be solved only by those with a wholly new mindset; those who are not right-brained or left-brained but who combine the two to create a type of thinking and perspective that simply can't be replicated by machines.

## SUMMARY

» Don't get distracted by symptoms.

» Survey the measurable feedback and focus on the facts.

» Always be ready.

# Day 11: Throw out your excuse book and always bring a solution

If you want to learn how to consistently bounce forward following a crisis or difficult times, you need to shift your focus from the problem to the solution. And that means throwing out your excuse book.

**HE THAT IS GOOD FOR MAKING EXCUSES IS SELDOM GOOD FOR ANYTHING ELSE.**
**– BENJAMIN FRANKLIN**

Whether we are facing personal or professional challenges, it's easy to blame some external force or person or circumstances outside our control. We lament the fact that we 'don't have time', yet the average person watches five hours of TV every day! At work the average worker is distracted by emails five times an hour. The Management Association has reported that the average employee spends 107 minutes each day on email, and we check social networking sites or news sites several times a day. We are wasting huge amounts of time while coming up with plausible excuses to justify poor performance.

In an effort to combat the excuse epidemic, I conducted a 'Throw Out Your Excuse Book' school tour. In each school I taped up the students' dominant hands and gave them a 24-hour challenge: they had to find a way to do what they normally did without access to excuses. The teachers loved it because no-one was allowed to make an excuse for a whole 24 hours.

Most of us don't realise how often we fall back on pat answers and excuses, so cut them out and demand that all the people in your life do the same. Instead focus on solutions.

It is important to recognise, however, that people who naturally seek problems and see the failings others miss are not always pessimists. Sometimes these individuals are crucial in a business. They can help to streamline manufacturing and can be incredibly useful for averting additional problems, but generally when you are in a crisis the last thing you need is 'Negative Norman' in the corner sniping about how you are all doomed.

As a rule, whether at home with your family or in a business, no-one should be encouraged to raise a problem unless they also bring at least one solution to that problem.

Problems are a huge source of opportunity if they are viewed from the right perspective. In the 1980s the business that would become Springfield Remanufacturing Corporation (SRC) was in trouble. Jack Stack and 12 of his management colleagues, with $100 000 of their own money and some additional funding, then bought the business from parent company International Harvester in a leveraged buy-out.

From near bankruptcy the company has since then created more than 35 separate companies that do everything from packaging to consulting to producing high-performance engines. And many of those new businesses have been created as a result of weaknesses or problems identified and solved by employees. SRC now has combined annual revenues of over $400 million and employs more than 1200 people. Bringing a positive mindset to problem- solving is a very profitable way to do business. And combining that with other key ideas we've covered already in this chapter can produce a very potent mix.

CEO Jack Stack may not have fully understood management and how to run a business when he took over SRC, but he did understand sport. His dream was to create a business using the same rules — a business where people had fun, played fair, kept score and had a voice. By giving everyone a share in the rewards Stack created an environment that self-regulated. If something wasn't right or a business unit faced a crisis, they collectively identified it and fixed it. The result, open-book management, has proved an extremely successful way of harnessing the inherent power of the team. Through an affiliated training business, The Great Game of Business, Stack now also teaches others how to apply the open-book management approach to emulate his results.

In short, he advocates that a business should be run like a game: set the rules, keep score, assign players, have fun and share the rewards. Every employee in SRC knows how to read a balance sheet; they have access to information and therefore understand what their decisions mean to the bottom line. Stock options and bonuses also mean that a large part of the equity in the business is distributed among the people who create it.

In a business crisis encourage everyone in the team to get involved and come up with potential solutions. When you implement these suggestions reward the person who came up with the idea. Don't get bogged down in creating incentive schemes or using money as a reward — it rarely works. Instead make sure you publicly thank the person who came up with the idea and everyone who was involved in its implementation. Gratitude and recognition are much greater motivators than money. If you would like to reward that person, then consider giving them a voucher for dinner for two at a lovely restaurant or some other experience they might enjoy.

## SUMMARY

» Focus on the solution not the problem.

» Don't waste time on justifications.

» Be grateful and give recognition where applicable.

# Day 12: Identify and use your strengths

The Greeks had a word — aretē — which meant functional goodness or virtue. So, for example, the aretē of an axe is to chop wood well, and the aretē of a paint brush is to apply paint well. Aristotle believed that all things and all people have a telos or purpose for which they are uniquely suited. Hungarian psychologist Mihaly Csikszentmihalyi drew on the same word when he defined his 'autotelic' moments. All the noise about 'talent' has pushed this idea into oblivion. Today when we talk about talent or natural strengths we have visions of participants on The X Factor and the resulting fame and fortune. We imagine sports stars or rock stars or artists or authors, but we all have telos and we all have arete — something we are uniquely, innately better at than most other people. It might not bring us fame or fortune but it can make us happier, more creative and positive. And considering that neither fame nor fortune has been demonstrated to make people happier, then perhaps it's time we recalibrated our ideas about talent and innate ability.

If you don't know what your signature strengths are, find out. I used the Clifton StrengthsFinder. I was first introduced to the system about eight months after my accident when someone recommended the book. I read the book and took the test and it revolutionised my life.

The Clifton StrengthsFinder is the life's work of Donald O. Clifton, a man described as the 'father of strengths-based psychology'. In the late 1990s Clifton was leading a team of Gallup scientists whose goal was to start a global conversation about what was right with people instead of what was wrong with them.

In the 1980s and most of the 1990s the focus in business was to identify individuals' weaknesses and have them work on those weaknesses until they became strengths. In fact, weakness intervention turned into a worldwide obsession and a multi-billion-dollar industry. But Clifton, along with others, thought this emphasis was misplaced.

In 1999 a book called *First, Break All the Rules* by Marcus Buckingham and Curt Coffman took the world by storm by documenting what the world's greatest managers did differently. Their source information came from two massive research studies spanning 25 years conducted by the Gallup Organization. Buckingham and Coffman identified four keys:

1. Select for talent.
2. Define the right outcome.
3. Focus on strengths.
4. Find the right fit.

While keys 1, 2 and 4 were no big surprise, the third key was. Up to that point most managers and leaders around the world believed their role was to work on and reduce weaknesses — both their own and other people's. Here was evidence-based research that demonstrated that this idea was just plain wrong.

The conclusion was you can't change people, at least not unless they want to change. So stop worrying about what skill was left out and focus all your attention on what was left in. Find ways to help that person recognise those gifts and use them as often as possible. Focus 'on each person's strengths and manage around his weaknesses. Don't try to fix the weaknesses. Don't try to perfect each person. Instead do everything you can to help each person cultivate his talents. Help each person become more of who he already is.'

Through the work of positive psychology pioneer Dr Martin Seligman, we already know that happiness consists of three components — pleasure, engagement and meaning. Pleasure is fleeting; engagement is facilitated by our depth of involvement with family, work, romantic relationships and hobbies; and meaning is derived from our personal strengths to serve a larger purpose. What we now understand is that finding and focusing on our strengths doesn't just make us more productive, it makes us much happier too.

The assessment tool the *Clifton StrengthsFinder* allows you to identify what those strengths are so you can recalibrate your life and work to ensure you use those gifts as often as possible throughout the day.

Based on a 40-year Gallup study of human strengths, Clifton created a language of the 34 most common talents and developed an assessment tool to help people discover and describe those talents. And you can take the assessment for under $10. It takes about 35 minutes to complete the questionnaire, then you will be sent your top five 'signature strengths' together with a report about what they mean.

My top five strengths are:

1.  Futurist

2.  Winning Others Over (WOO)

3.  Communication

4.  Positivity

5.  Strategic.

'Futurist' means I am inspired by the future and its possibilities. I also love working with kids and inspiring others to consider what their future could be like. My speaking and consulting career now allows me to do this. Later, in the afterword, I'll touch on the work we're doing in India with our foundation to help change other people's futures for the better.

'Winning others over' means I love the challenge of meeting and helping to motivate people, and again my speaking career has allowed me to meet some really interesting and inspiring people. I collect friends like some people collect stamps! I just love meeting new people and making new connections.

'Communication' means I generally find it easy to put my thoughts into words. My speaking career taps into this strength because I love presenting and firing up new conversations with others. Even this book is a form of communication that has been fun.

'Positivity' means my enthusiasm is contagious. I'm upbeat, regardless of what life throws at me, and again my career allows me to use this strength to encourage others who are going through difficult times to bounce forward instead of back.

Finally, I'm 'strategic' because I can always find an alternative way to proceed. This is particularly useful in my corporate coaching work, because I can help others see the wood for the trees and forge a new path out of difficulty.

You can pay more than $10 to access the full list of 34 of your Clifton StrengthsFinder results so you can identify your top ten strengths and your biggest weaknesses, but I chose to focus on my top five. Now I manage my life around those strengths, ensuring that I spend the vast majority of my time using one or more of them. I'm happy, productive and excited about life as a result, and perhaps more importantly I get to honour the three challenges I put to myself when I was at the crash site waiting for the ambulance:

» Was I PASSIONATE toward my family, living a full life?

» Was I PRODUCTIVE in my life, my career, my dreams, my purpose?

» Was I MAKING A DIFFERENCE in others' lives, adding value to the world, creating a legacy?

By taking the time to identify my strengths I know that every day I am passionate. I am living life to the full because I'm doing what I was born to do. I am productive because I'm loving what I'm doing — it's not a chore. I still work ridiculous hours and I have millions of frequent flyer points, but I'm passionate, productive and I'm making a difference. My life has meaning because I'm using my strengths to add value.

Whatever crisis you face you need to stop, take stock and put yourself and the other people in your team in the right spot. I would strongly recommend that your people do the Clifton StrengthsFinder and use those insights to find appropriate solutions to your business challenges. Be open and flexible and allow people to trade parts of their jobs with each other so more people are doing more of what they are good at.

Gallup research has already proven the worth of strengths-based leadership. For example, Gallup found that only one-third of more than 10 million people surveyed from around the world agreed with the statement, 'At work, I have the opportunity to do what I do best every day.' Is it really any wonder that the statistics on workforce disengagement are so terrible? Remember the McKinsey & Company report that in some countries as few as 2 to 3 percent of employees are actively engaged in the work they do every day.

What a waste!

Gallup studies have also found that people who have the opportunity to do what they are best at every day are six times as likely to be engaged in their jobs and more than three times as likely to report having an excellent quality of life.

Business leaders, in crisis and out, need to take notice of strengths and help individuals to use them consistently, because when they do amazing things are possible for everyone. Productivity, positivity, creativity and happiness increase and from that mindset anything is possible.

The same is true of a career crisis. Step back and really assess what it is you are good at and enjoy. Sometimes we can be blinded by our own experience and fail to see that many of our strengths are transferable across a number of different professions. If you are facing a career crisis, whether you can't seem to progress or you've been made redundant, use the space to pull back the veil and look at what really makes you tick. Often we fall into a profession because it's the first job we secure and then stay there because that's where our experience lies. But every role has elements that will be just as useful in another profession. Finding out what your strengths are will help you to position yourself for a new role, to redefine your role to become more productive or to change career completely.

The Clifton StrengthsFinder was a really powerful assessment tool for me but it's by no means the only one available. Among others, you might also consider the Instinctive Drive (ID) system or the Myers-Briggs Type Indicator (MBTI).

Instinctive Drive is a fantastic tool that helps to unravel the 'why' behind your behaviour, which can then allow you to organise your life in a way that supports your instinctive drives. This will allow you to get into your own natural groove instead of fighting against the grain all the time. After answering a short questionnaire you are assigned a four-number code, which identifies a specific combination of the four main instinctive drives, Verify, Authenticate, Complete and Improvise, to indicate your innate operating system. Knowing this can help you work out how to get the best from yourself and others.

The Myers-Briggs Type Indicator, or MBTI, assesses our behaviours and how best we work together based on personality characteristics. MBTI looks specifically at how we see the world, make decisions and organise activities.

Not every crisis can be sorted in 12 days — far from it. But if you have completed the 12-day challenge described in this chapter you will be well on your way to bouncing forward.

# Conclusion
## The power of bounce

I can honestly say I wouldn't change a thing in my life. There have been highs and there have been terrible lows. My accident tested me to the limit of my physical endurance, and losing my brother David was even harder to bear. But these experiences and many others are what define me — they've made me the man I am today.

My accident changed my life but what really transformed it was my determination to use the crisis to create an even better life than I had enjoyed before. Just three years after my accident I learned that I'd been nominated as the 2009 Tasmanian Young Australian of the Year. A number of friends had put my name forward and I thought, what an honour just to be nominated. I went to the ceremony, though I didn't think I had much chance of winning, especially after reading what everyone else had achieved. So you can imagine my surprise when they announced I had won. People respond to stories of adversity because they remind us of what we are all really capable of and they inspire us, even if only for a moment, to think impossible thoughts about our own life.

As the state winner I was invited along with other award winners to meet the Prime Minister of Australia at the time, Kevin Rudd, at his home. Mr Rudd was introduced to the various guests including cricket legends Glenn McGrath and Adam Gilchrist. As Glenn stepped aside I moved forward and thrust out my prosthetic hand for Mr Rudd to shake . . . and without warning him I then disconnected it from its support so that as he shook my hand it came off in his! For a moment there was silence and I almost thought to myself, 'Oh no! What have I done! I've just played a prank on the Prime Minister!' But then he started laughing and everyone else realised what I'd done and started laughing too.

News of my prank travelled fast and appeared in all the national newspapers. People were talking about it on the radio, on television. I had people ringing me to arrange interviews and wanting me to give comment on 'The Young Australian of the Year's 'armless prank on the prime minister'. The story even appeared in *The New York Times*! I'd wanted to do something that would make Kevin Rudd remember me and, wow, I definitely managed that!

From that point onwards my speaking business exploded! Overnight I was in the public eye and was being approached to speak at big events. Today I speak all over the world. By my best calculation I speak to about 100000 people a year. I've also worked with global brands such as Google, ExxonMobil, BP and Citibank, to name just a few.

Since my accident I've been fitted with the most advanced bionic arm in the world. Produced by the European company Touch Bionics, and worth close to $100 000, it enables me to move each finger and program it with my iPhone through Bluetooth. It feels amazing and has certainly made life a little easier, but I don't wear it all the time. I have accepted my disability but it doesn't hold me back. Not now, not ever.

The world isn't fair at times. Too many bad things happen to too many good people. Bereavement, cancer, chronic illness, heart attack, military combat, natural disaster, physical assault, refugee displacement — these are among the very worst things that can befall us, yet research has found that every one of these adversities can spur massive emotional growth and become the catalyst for many successes. Crisis can take endless forms in business too. Lost accounts, changing legislation, diminishing market share, fraud, loss of reputation — the list is endless. But again some people turn these difficulties into opportunities and forge ahead into a bright new future.

Forget what others think or say. You may not be able to control all the elements of your future but with the right mindset you can exert far more control over the outcomes than you imagine.

They told me I'd never walk again. They told Kate and me that we would never have children. They told me I'd never be able to play the guitar again. I'm walking, we have a beautiful family and I still play the guitar.

## THERE IS NO EDUCATION LIKE ADVERSITY.
## – BENJAMIN DISRAELI

Did you know that a group of rhinos is called a 'crash'? The collective name can probably be explained by the fact that they have very poor eyesight and can only see about nine metres in front of them but they can run at over 45 km per hour. Needless to say they crash into and through many things.

I can relate to a crash of rhinos, and not just because we share a life experience. I love that they can't really see the future but it doesn't faze them or diminish their courage. Like the rhinoceros, it doesn't matter how many obstructions or barriers we encounter in life, how many times we crash into things or suffer setbacks, we can always pick ourselves up and continue to bounce forward.

# Afterword

A great deal has happened since I first wrote *Bounce Forward*. Not only did the book help put me on the map as a professional speaker but more importantly, readers loved the message and seemed to really resonate with the idea that crisis didn't have to be an end point but, with the right mindset and methodology, it could simply be the start of something new. We all face crisis moments in our life. Mine occurred when my Holden V8 Statesman sedan ploughed into a truck leading to months in hospital and life changing injuries. For others, it might be the end of a relationship, the demise of a business, the loss of a friend or child. Life sucks sometimes and that is true for all of us regardless of wealth, geography, race, colour or creed. Too often we instinctively believe these moments are negative and that life will never be as good again.

This is almost never true — not if we *Bounce Forward*. Our lives may never be the same but we rarely entertain the possibility that life may actually be even better. It doesn't often even cross our minds that something amazing, beautiful or even unexpected may rise from the ashes like a phoenix from the frames.

By the time I wrote the book I'd already *Bounced Forward* into an almost unrecognizable life. Even then I thought it was a one-time deal. Little did I know that my bouncing was far from over.

The unexpected outcome of writing this book and the increase in speaking engagements it facilitated was that as well as connecting to the message and my story, people were curious about how I became a speaker. I was really humbled by some of the stories I heard — incredible obstacles that people had surmounted, tragedy people had endured but gone on to thrive as well as countless other stories. It was clear to me that these stories should also be shared because they could help others and these individuals could be professional speakers — they just didn't realise it yet. I started to help a few people to clarify their message and shape their story so that it landed with people and really delivered value to their audience. Before long, these people were doing well and getting speaking gigs, often crediting me with helping them through the training and advice I had given. And that made me think ... was there any professional speaker training programs in Australia? Was there any training anywhere in the world?

No one was training professional speakers, certainly none that I could see and certainly not to a sufficiently high level of development and polish. The result, I *Bounced Forward* again and became the CEO and founder of the Speakers Institute.

The mission was simple: To transform leaders to become influential speakers.

Since it's inception, the *Speakers Institute* has offered a world class curriculum, helping would-be speakers design, refine and deliver their message with clarity, conviction and passion.

» We are training over 6000 speakers from around the world each year.

» Our students go on to do TEDx Talks, get highly paid international speaking engagements and impact audiences every day with their messages, stories and knowledge.

» Many of our students become influencers, write a book and are featured in the media for their advice and opinions.

- » We work with some of the largest organisations in the world including Google, Canon, IBM and Gallup.

- » We run over 30 live events each month in many countries with our HQ in Sydney, Australia.

- » We have many programs in which we train within, from evening events, one day programs, 3-day experiences and 18-month immersions.

- » Most of our products are based around 'How to Master Communication for Influence'.

- » We have reached more than 170 million people directly and indirectly and our online reach is over one million people per year.

- » As of mid-2019, the business, which now involves a large team, has grown over 100% year on year placing us in the top 20 of Australia's fastest growing companies.

And, all of this has come about on the back of having a car accident. First by learning how to communicate that story really powerfully to offer a message of hope and resilience to others. Then teaching other people how they can also overcome their own adversity and go on and share their stories with other people — how to master communication for influence, possibly even as a professional speaker. All this great stuff has directly or indirectly come from one of the worst moments of my life. Even in my wildest dreams I couldn't have imagined this was possible.

Today, the core of my work is influence. I am super passionate about teaching people how to positively influence others through story. But not through storytelling but through *storyshowing*. My next book after *Bounce Forward* was *Storyshowing: How to Stand Out from the Storytellers*, also published by Wiley. It was released in 2017 as an instruction manual for making an emotional connection through story. Again, the book really hit a nerve with readers. I am constantly humbled by the feedback and how the book and the courses we run through the Speakers Institute have transformed lives. There is nothing more magical than helping people who have their own powerful stories to tell find their voice so that they can arrive at a place of confidence and go on to help their own audiences in the future. It's a powerful idea, and a powerful movement of influencers changing the world one message at a time.

## I DON'T TELL TO INFORM; I EMOTIONALLY SHOW TO TRANSFORM.
## – SAM CAWTHORN

When we come to realise that our mess is often our message, that our life may never be the same as it was due to some kairos moment but the challenge and sense of injustice we initially feel can and does pass to give way to a new path and a new purpose. The truth is our moment of crisis not only impacts us in ways we might not immediately appreciate but our experiences can also be the catalyst for change for others. Our hardships and challenges take on new meaning because they offer new insights or perspectives to the wider world. My passion is helping people get those stories out to the world.

Life is never linear or smooth or unaffected by bumps in the road. We are all called on our own Hero's Journey and sharing that journey is both part of the healing and part of the metamorphosis into something new that offers greater value to others. For me that Hero's Journey has been present all along. My life before the accident, my kairos moment on the highway and then my life today and how the accident has really shaped and defined my purpose and destiny. I am now the living embodiment of how I have *Bounced Forward*, not just from a physical point of view but a career point of view. I am now doing what I believe I was put on this earth to do. And this is true for all of us — crisis is often the light that illuminates that purpose. Helping others to appreciate that fact is my life's work. What have your moments of crisis shown you? Have you got a message that needs to be shared? What have you learned that could be helpful for others?

When each of us reach that point of appreciation and have *Bounced Forward* in some way our story is no longer ours to own. The onus is on us to share our Hero's Journey with others so that others can be helped by our crisis which in turn can encourage them to *Bounce Forward* and repeat the process.

I would love to hear how you have Bounced Forward and used the challenging times you've faced to carve our a new life and encourage others to face their own difficulties with optimism that something even better could be just around the corner.

**bounceforward@samcawthorn.com**

Perhaps, your next step should be to contact the Speakers Institutue and get your Bounce Forward story out there.

As for me, my next step is a new book ...

## The Profile Economy: How to win in the future of influence

This movement of influence with people sharing their stories to help others really is an idea whose time has come. Today people follow people. Even if we look back to the 'noughties', people followed and paid attention to brands, businesses, companies, logos, products and governments. That has all changed and we now see people following people. Now 90% of online followers are following people. Often those people started off like you and me with something to say or something to share whether that was how to use yoga to heal, how to master the art of make-up, filming practical jokes or sharing their knowledge, opinion or story in some way. 92% of all the content consumed online is now written by individuals who want to share their opinion, their depth of experience and knowledge, add a comment or simply share their own story. This is very different from the company or government led communication of the past.

We all have knowledge and experiences that other people don't know but could benefit from. That makes all our stories valuable which is exactly what I've been saying for years! Simon Sinek put it beautifully when he said, 'People don't buy what you do, they buy why you do it'. We all have a why. The 'how' is the Hero's Journey that often brings that why to the surface. In other words, we all have a story and now we have the platform to share that story whether from the stage by being a professional speaker or by becoming a blogger, vlogger or other online influencer. It's never been easier to develop a profile and win the future of influence.

My next book and my next *Bounce Forward* will be around encouraging people to own that space to develop their online and offline profile to help others and how that can be converted into a commercial income stream.

Together, we can all keep bouncing ...

THE BEST IS YET TO COME!